What people are saying

"Here at Citibank we use the Quick Course® co
for 'just-in-time' job aids—the books are great foɪ ᴜᴏᴇɪᴏ wɪio are too busy for
tutorials and training. Quick Course® books provide very clear instruction
and easy reference."

Bill Moreno, Development Manager
Citibank
San Francisco, CA

"At Geometric Results, much of our work is PC related and we need training
tools that can quickly and effectively improve the PC skills of our people.
Early this year we began using your materials in our internal PC training
curriculum and the results have been outstanding. Both participants and
instructors like the books and the measured learning outcomes have been very
favorable."

Roger Hill, Instructional Systems Designer
Geometric Results Incorporated
Southfield, MI

"The concise and well organized text features numbered instructions, screen
shots, and useful quick reference pointers, and tips…[This] affordable text is
very helpful for educators who wish to build proficiency."

Computer Literacy column
Curriculum Administrator Magazine
Stamford, CT

"I have purchased five other books on this subject that I've probably paid
more than $60 for, and your [Quick Course®] book taught me more than those
five books combined!"

Emory Majors
Searcy, AR

"I would like you to know how much I enjoy the Quick Course® books I have
received from you. The directions are clear and easy to follow with attention
paid to every detail of the particular lesson."

Betty Weinkauf, Retired Senior
Mission, TX

QUICK COURSE®

in

MICROSOFT® WINDOWS NT 4

Workstation

ONLINE PRESS INC.

Microsoft® Press

PUBLISHED BY
Microsoft Press
A Division of Microsoft Corporation
One Microsoft Way
Redmond, WA 98052-6399

Library of Congress Cataloging-in-Publication Data

Quick Course in Microsoft Windows NT Workstation 4 / Online Press
    Inc.
        p.   cm.
    Includes index.
    ISBN 1-57231-843-0
        1. Microsoft Windows NT.   2. Operating systems (Computers)
    3. Microcomputer workstations.   I. Online Press Inc.
    QA76.76.O63Q523   1997
    005.4'469- -dc21   97-41169
                                                            CIP

Printed and bound in the United States of America.

1 2 3 4 5 6 7 8 9   QMQM   2 1 0 9 8 7

Distributed to the book trade in Canada by Macmillan of Canada, a division of Canada Publishing Corporation.

A CIP record of this book is available from the British Library.

Microsoft Press books are available through booksellers and distributors worldwide. For further information about international editions, contact your local Microsoft Corporation office. Or contact Microsoft Press International directly at fax (425) 936-7329. Visit our Web site at mspress.microsoft.com.

A Quick Course® Education/Training Edition for this title is published by Online Press Inc. For information about supplementary workbooks, contact Online Press Inc. at 14320 NE 21st St., Suite 18, Bellevue, WA, 98007, USA, 1-800-854-3344.

Authors: Joyce Cox of Online Press Inc. and Richard Cooper, a network specialist and co-owner of MicroAge Computer Center, Bellevue, Washington
Reviewer: Brad Gjerding, a computer and engineering systems analyst with Seattle Pacific University, Seattle, Washington
Acquisitions Editor: Susanne M. Freet
Project Editor: Maureen Williams Zimmerman

From the publisher

"I love these books!"

I can't tell you the number of times people have said those exact words to me about our new Quick Course® software training book series. And when I ask them what makes the books so special, this is what they say:

- **They're short and approachable, but they give you hours worth of good information.**

  Written for busy people with limited time, most Quick Course books are designed to be completed in 15 to 40 hours. Because Quick Course books are usually divided into two parts—Learning the Basics and Building Proficiency—users can selectively choose the chapters that meet their needs and complete them as time allows.

- **They're relevant and fun, and they assume you're no dummy.**

  Written in an easy-to-follow, step-by-step format, Quick Course books offer streamlined instruction for the new user in the form of no-nonsense, to-the-point tutorials and learning exercises. Each book provides a logical sequence of instructions for creating useful business documents—the same documents people use on the job. People can either follow along directly or substitute their own information and customize the documents. After finishing a book, users have a valuable "library" of documents they can continually recycle and update with new information.

- **They're direct and to the point, and they're a lot more than just pretty pictures.**

  Training-oriented rather than feature-oriented, Quick Course books don't cover the things you don't really need to know to do useful work. They offer easy-to-follow, step-by-step instructions; lots of screen shots for checking work in progress; quick-reference pointers for fast, easy lookup and review; and useful tips offering additional information on topics being discussed.

- **They're a rolled-into-one-book solution, and they meet a variety of training needs.**

  Designed with instructional flexibility in mind, Quick Course books can be used both for self-training and as the basis for weeklong courses, two-day seminars, and all-day workshops. They can be adapted to meet a variety of training needs, including classroom instruction, take-away practice exercises, and self-paced learning.

Microsoft Press is very excited about bringing you this extraordinary series. But you must be the judge. I hope you'll give these books a try. And maybe the next time I see you, you too will say, "Hey, Jim! I love these books!"

Jim Brown, Publisher
Microsoft Press

Content overview

Content details

ONE

LEARNING THE BASICS

In Part One, we cover basic techniques for working with Windows NT Workstation 4. After you complete these four chapters, you'll know enough to be able to accomplish daily tasks. In Chapter 1, you learn about operating systems and networks, start NT, and become familiar with the desktop. In Chapter 2, you use some of the programs that come with NT as you give commands and work with multiple programs. In Chapter 3, you find and open files, and you create folders and get organized. In Chapter 4, after a discussion of network security, you access network resources, including printers.

1

Introducing
Windows NT Workstation 4

We set the stage with a discussion of some important operating-system and network concepts. Then
we start Windows NT Workstation 4 and explore the
desktop, icons, and windows. We also show you how
to get help.

Access resources by double-clicking icons

Manually move and size windows for the best view

Use buttons to expand and contract windows and close programs

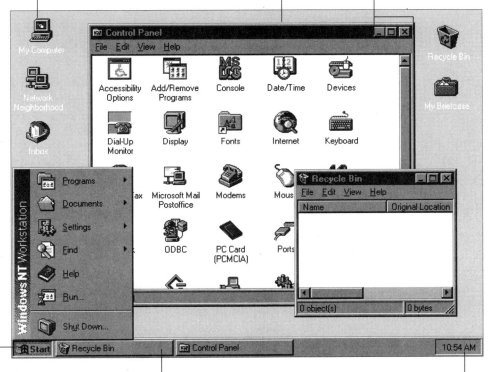

Access resources by choosing them from the Start menu

Check the taskbar to know which programs are open

Use the clock to keep track of time

Microsoft Windows NT Workstation 4 is a set of programs that together comprise your computer's *operating system*. This operating system controls how all the parts of your computer work together to perform specific tasks, and provides a set of tools that give you a visual way of telling your computer what to do. Because we assume that Windows NT Workstation is already installed on your computer, we don't go into the details of installation in this book. Instead, we focus on what you need to know about NT to do useful work. We do give some background information for new computer users, but those of you who are new to NT but not new to computers can simply skim over those sections.

Why Do You Need an Operating System?

So what exactly is an operating system and why do you need one? Your computer's operating system coordinates all your *hardware* (the central processing unit or CPU, memory, hard drives, floppy drives, CD-ROM drives, monitor, keyboard, mouse, and any other devices) by means of *software* (computer programs). When you work on your computer, you work with two kinds of software: application programs and system programs.

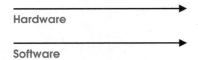
Hardware

Software

- **Application programs.** You use these programs to perform specific types of tasks. For example, you can construct spreadsheet models with spreadsheet programs such as Microsoft Excel, and you can write reports with word-processing programs such as Microsoft Word. On the surface, a spreadsheet program and a word-processing program might seem very different, but many functions are common to both types of program. For example, both need to respond to keyboard instructions, retrieve files from a hard drive or floppy drive, show the information in files on-screen, change the information, and save it on disk. Each application could provide its own instructions for these routine tasks, but long ago software developers realized it would be more efficient to have one set of programs carry out these basic functions for all other programs.

- **System programs.** These programs were developed to perform common functions, and collections of system programs designed to work together became known as an operating system. By managing files and hardware devices and overseeing basic system operations, an operating system provides a foundation for the application programs that are designed to work with, or *run under*, it. That way, as long as the developers of application programs make sure their programs work with the operating system, they don't have to worry about making them work with every kind of CPU, every kind of monitor, every kind of sound card, and so on.

What's the Big Deal About NT?

Windows NT Workstation 4 is one of a series of operating systems from Microsoft Corporation, and it offers some distinct advantages over its predecessors. These advantages are winning more and more converts among corporations, government agencies, and educational institutions, but they also appeal to many individual computer users. If you bought Windows NT Workstation 4 and installed it on your own computer, you already know why. But if, like most people, you are simply using the operating system supplied by your organization, you might want to know some of the factors that influenced the decision to go with NT.

- **Graphical user interface (GUI).** Pronounced *gooey,* this fancy term just means that you can carry out tasks visually by using onscreen pictures called *icons* instead of having to type instructions in some obscure operating-system language. Organizations generally like GUIs because they are supposed to be more intuitive and easier to learn to use. These days, GUIs are old hat, but one of the important features of Windows NT Workstation 4 is that it uses the sophisticated GUI of Windows 95 (another member of Microsoft's operating-system family). In fact, the superficial look and feel of NT is almost identical to that of Windows 95 (there are some subtle differences). Beneath the surface, however, NT is entirely different, with the speed, stability, and security needed to manage huge files on huge networks without collapsing under the pressure.

Easy to use

Flexible →
- **Networking capabilities.** Built into NT are the programs necessary for computers to work with one another. We talk more about networks on page 7, but briefly, NT not only enables computers of the same type to interact but also acts as a sort of bridge between different computer types, called *platforms*. For example, with NT the people working on Intel-based PCs in the sales department can talk to the people working on Macintoshes in the advertising department.

Fast →
- **Speed.** NT moves information 32 bits at a time. So what? Well, that's twice as much information as older-generation operating systems, which could move only 16 bits at once. (Of course, this extra muscle gets a workout only if the programs running under NT also move 32 bits at a time, but you can see the potential.) NT can also work with computers with more than one processor, making it attractive to computer-speed freaks.

Dependable →
- **Stability.** In this case, *stable* means *dependable*, as in *less likely to crash*. NT manages your programs' use of memory in such a way that one malfunctioning program doesn't freeze up the entire system.

Secure →
- **Security.** Because NT guards all the gates to your computer's hardware, it can completely control who can do what with which file or which device, both on a specific workstation and on the network as a whole. So corporations and governments can store sensitive information on the computer without fear of it being viewed or used by unauthorized people. One of these security mechanisms is a file storage system known as *NTFS*. We delve into the topic of security on page 92 and discuss NTFS in a tip on page 95.

Hardware compatiblity

To see if your computer and its peripherals are compatible with NT 4, first check the *Hardware Compatiblity List*, a 170-page book packaged with the NT software. If any of your hardware is not in this book, it might still be compatible because new hardware is continually being tested and added to the list. You can obtain the latest version of the list from Microsoft's Web site at *www.microsoft.com/ntserver/hcl/-hclintro.htm.*

NT does have some disadvantages. First, it doesn't work with all hardware components (see the adjacent tip). Second, it doesn't work with all programs—only with those that play according to its rules. Many programs developed to run under MS-DOS, Windows 3.*x*, and Windows 95 will run just fine under NT, but others—particularly those that want to talk directly to your hardware—may be unreliable or may not run at all.

What's a Network?

You might be running Windows NT Workstation 4 on a *stand-alone computer*—a single machine that is not connected to any other computer. Or your computer might be connected to a *network*—a bunch of other computers that might be physically located in one building or scattered in different buildings or even different parts of the world. Networks can be intimidating. At their simplest, they involve cards, cables, and software, and at their most complex, they involve sophisticated hardware and satellite communications. They require planning before they're installed and ongoing maintenance after they're installed. But fortunately, none of that needs to concern you. If you are connected to a network, a *network administrator* is most likely responsible for setting it up and keeping it running, not you. All you need to worry about is learning how to use NT and the network to carry out basic tasks.

The whole point of networking is usually to share *resources.* What's a resource? Anything that you or the other people on your network use can be a resource. Here are a few examples:

- **Files.** On a network, files used by more than one person can be stored in a central location. Some people may be allowed to work with the files, others may be allowed to view them, and still others may not be allowed to access them at all.

- **Hardware.** Printers, modems, and other similar bits of hardware that are attached to one computer can be used by other computers.

- **Backup systems.** Information stored on multiple computers can be backed up to a single backup device, such as a large hard drive, a tape drive, or an optical disk drive.

- **Information.** You can send electronic messages, coordinate schedules, and communicate "on the spot" with your colleagues—all without leaving your desk. As a result, group projects are easier to plan and execute, without the necessity of face-to-face meetings.

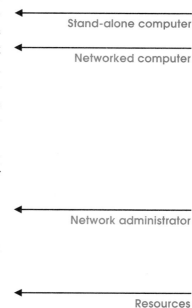

Stand-alone computer

Networked computer

Network administrator

Resources

By the time you finish this book, you'll be comfortable using some or all of these resources and will take the benefits offered by your network and NT for granted.

Who's Responsible for What?

Obviously, if you are running NT on a stand-alone computer, you are responsible for the whole shebang. You can use any installed program you want, store your files where you want, and "decorate" your computer screen any way you want.

Types of networks

Your level of responsibility for a networked computer depends on whether the network is peer-to-peer or client-server:

- **Peer-to-peer networks.** These networks are appropriate for small groups of computers (suggested for up to ten) that all have equal status. The computers may have different network functions—for example, a computer connected to a shared printer will probably be the print server for the entire network—and one user on the network may be responsible for adding or removing hardware and trouble-shooting network problems. But by and large, each user controls his or her own resources, and the network functions pretty democratically.

- **Client-server networks.** These networks are appropriate for large groups of computers and any group for which data security is important. A powerful *server computer* running the Microsoft Windows NT Server operating system is connected to a set of *client computers* and controls what the clients can do. (Large organizations usually have more than one server.) How the server controls its clients is determined by the person designated as the network administrator (or *system administrator*), who has overall responsibility for the network and has dictatorial powers. Depending on the nature of the company and its data, this benevolent dictator may delegate some of his or her powers to the users of client computers, allowing them to control the programs and files on their own computers and to customize their machines to suit their work habits. Or the network administrator may need to maintain strict control of all aspects of the network and its resources.

Why does all this concern you? Because while you are working your way through this book, you might find you can't access a file, run a program, or perform a task according to our instructions. You haven't done anything wrong, and we haven't goofed. Your computer simply doesn't have *permission* to do what you're trying to do. (See page 93 for more information about permissions.) Just make a note in the margin of the book, skip that section, and move on to the next. (If you think you ought to be able to perform that task, talk to your network administrator.)

◀────────────── IMPORTANT

What's Your Name?

As you'll find out while reading this book, NT requires you to enter various names and passwords to use a networked computer. Usually someone else has decided what the names and passwords are and simply hands them to you. But sometimes you will need to change a password. (We explain how in the adjacent tip.) Here are some of the names and passwords you may encounter:

- **Your computer name.** Each computer has a unique computer name that identifies it for other computers on your network.

- **Your domain or workgroup name.** If the computer is part of the domain, you need to know the domain name. If it is part of a workgroup within the domain, you need to know the workgroup name. This name is like a club membership. (See page 93 for more information.)

- **Your user name.** When you start NT, you must *log on* or identify yourself to the network by entering your user name and password.

- **Resource names.** Each shared resource, such as a printer, has a resource name and may have a password that controls access to it.

- **Your e-mail name.** If you can send and receive e-mail, you have an e-mail name, or *address*, that identifies the "mailbox" where your e-mail is stored. To get at the messages in your mailbox, you must enter this e-mail name and a password.

What you need to know about passwords

Your network administrator can control when you must change your user password. You may be required to change your password after you log on for the first time or after a certain period of time. You may be allowed to change the password whenever you want, change it only after a certain number of days, or never change it. You may be forced to choose a password that uses at least a certain number of characters or to choose a new one every time you make a change (not one you have used before). If you have any questions, check with your network administrator. When you need to change your password, press Ctrl+Alt+Delete to display the Windows NT Security dialog box, click Change Password, type your old password, type the new one, confirm the new one, click OK, and then click Cancel.

How do you keep everything straight? On well-designed networks, the naming scheme is simple and intuitive, and many names may have been set up for you when Windows NT Workstation 4 was installed on your computer. Passwords are another matter. They are an integral part of system security and the more obscure they are, and the more often they change, the better. (We talk more about system security on page 92.) You have no option but to memorize passwords, because writing them on bits of paper and leaving them in obvious places defeats the entire purpose of having passwords (and will undoubtedly incur the wrath of your network administrator).

We assume that your network administrator has given you the names and passwords you need. Check with him or her if you don't have this information.

Starting Windows NT Workstation 4

Without any more preamble, let's fire up NT. To complete the following steps, you need to know your user name and password, and the name of your domain or workgroup if you belong to one. You'll enter this information in a dialog box. We talk more about dialog boxes on page 37, but for now, simply follow our instructions:

1. Turn on your computer. Your computer runs a series of tests to ensure that all the parts of your computer are working correctly. Then you are asked to select which operating system you want to use for this work session.

What's a default?

Almost every operation in NT has a default, which is the action NT will carry out if you don't specify a different one. Pressing Enter in step 2 (adjacent) implements this default. If you are presented with a set of options and you don't know which to pick, often the safest thing to do is to stick with the default option suggested by NT.

2. If Windows NT Workstation Version 4.00 is selected, press Enter to accept this default or wait a few seconds for NT to proceed on its own. If it's not selected, press the Up Arrow or Down Arrow key to select it, and then press Enter. Either way, NT starts, and after a flurry of activity, you see this Begin Logon dialog box:

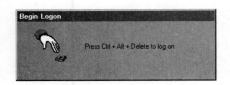

3. Hold down both the Ctrl and Alt keys, press the Delete key, and release all the keys at once. (We'll use a phrase like *Press Ctrl+Alt+Delete* when we want you to use a combination of keys to perform an action.) If you are working on a client-server network, you then see a dialog box like this one:

The User Name and Domain boxes may contain the names entered for the previous session or they may be empty. (Your

What happens before NT starts?

Windows NT Workstation 4 can't do its operating-system thing if your hardware is not working correctly or if any of its files are missing or damaged. So before NT starts, your computer's components and the necessary files are checked. First comes a Power On Self Test (POST), which checks your hardware, including memory. During the POST, you will probably see several hardware-related messages on your screen. Then what happens depends on what type of computer you are working on. If you are working on a PC, your computer's Basic Input Output System (BIOS), which is a program permanently stored on a chip on your computer's motherboard, looks for a startup disk, which is a disk that contains a Master Boot Record program. The BIOS first checks whether a startup disk is inserted in your floppy drive. (That's why the light on your floppy drive comes on briefly during the startup process.) If the drive contains a disk that is not a startup disk, you see a message telling you to remove the disk and press any key on your keyboard to continue the search. Then the BIOS checks your main hard drive. When it finds the Master Boot Record, it loads that program into memory. This behind-the-scenes process is slightly different if you are working on a RISC-based computer, but the result is basically the same. You see more messages on the screen, until finally, a boot loader program clears the screen and displays the message *OS Loader V4.0* and allows you to select an operating system, including *Windows NT Workstation Version 4.00*. (On PCs, one of the options presented is *Windows NT Workstation Version 4.00 (VGA mode)*. Why? So that if NT doesn't like your video card and you have problems with the display, you can restart the computer in simple VGA mode, which works with most cards and monitors. You can then continue working on your computer while you or your network administrator figure out what the problems is.) After you select the operating system, you see the message *Press spacebar now to invoke Hardware Profile/Last Known Good menu*. Usually you will simply do nothing at this point. The screen changes color and after a short pause, you see the Begin Logon dialog box shown on the facing page. However, if you have had trouble starting NT on your computer after adding or removing a component, you can press the Spacebar when you see the *Press spacebar now to invoke Hardware Profile/Last Known Good menu* message, and then press the L key to start NT with the Last Known Good configuration—the one used the last time you started NT successfully. Any changes you have made to the configuration since then will be discarded, and you can begin trying to track down the problem.

network administrator can specify that the entries from the previous session should not be retained.) Instead of a Domain box, you may have a Workgroup box.

If you are working on a peer-to-peer network or a stand-alone computer, your dialog box looks like the one below because you are the administrator of this system, and the workgroup you belong to is specified elsewhere:

If you do nothing, after a while the dialog box disappears and, as a security precaution, is replaced by the Begin Logon dialog box. You then have to press Ctrl+Alt+Delete again.

4. If necessary, double-click the entry in the User Name edit box and type your own user name.

5. Press Tab to move to the Password edit box, and type your password. For security reasons, the password is not displayed as you type it. Instead, a series of asterisks helps you keep track of how many characters you have typed. You must type the password exactly, including capitalization.

Why do you have to press Ctrl+Alt+Delete?

Why doesn't NT display the Logon Information dialog box right away? So that hackers can't use a program to display a fake dialog box and steal your name and password. Pressing Ctrl+Alt+Delete clears your computer's memory of any programs that shouldn't be there and ensures that the Logon Information dialog box you see is the one displayed by NT.

What if you forget your password?

If you forget your password, ask your network administrator to assign you a new one. Once you know the new password, you can log on to your computer and then change the password, if necessary. Unfortunately, the network administrator cannot look up your existing password; he or she can only delete an old one and assign a new one.

What happens if you make a mistake?

If you make a mistake when you enter your password and your computer "locks up," your network administrator has probably set some lockout options. These options tell your computer to stop responding after a certain number of failed logon attempts. If this happens, contact your administrator so that he or she can tell you what course of action to take.

6. If necessary, press Tab to move to the Domain or Workgroup edit box, and type your domain or workgroup name.

7. Click OK.

That's all there is to it. NT verifies that a user with your name and password is authorized to work on this computer, and you then see a screen that looks something like this one:

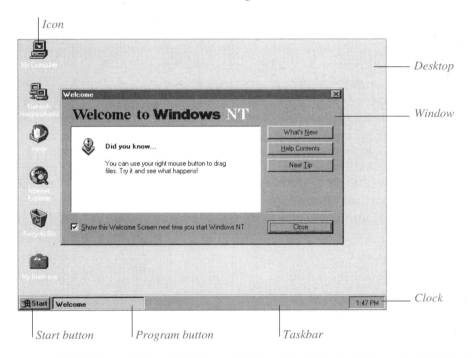

Icon

Desktop

Window

Clock

Start button   Program button   Taskbar

Switching from Windows or Windows for Workgroups?

You might think that knowing Windows or Windows for Workgroups 3.x will give you a jump start on getting down to work with Windows NT Workstation 4, but it seems that totally novice computer users often learn basic techniques faster than former Windows or Windows for Workgroups users. Why? Because they don't spend time looking for the equivalents of old Windows components such as Program Manager and File Manager. They focus on what they want to do and how they can do it with NT, instead of constantly translating to and from old Windows. If you are an old Windows hand, you may find it easier to come up to speed with the new operating system if you approach the learning of NT with an open mind and if, at least initially, you resist the temptation to compare the new operating system with the old Windows interface.

Initial capital letters

In this book, you'll notice that sometimes the option names we use don't exactly match those you see on the screen. We always capitalize the first letter of every word so that you won't stumble when you see the option names in a sentence. For example, on page 17 we tell you to click By Name, when the option on the screen is by Name. See what we mean? When both words start with a capital letter, they stand out better, don't they?

The Desktop

NT's opening screen is known as the *desktop*. This well-worn metaphor is designed to make using the tools available with NT no more intimidating than using the tools found on a typical desk in a typical office. If you are already familiar with Windows 95, you'll instantly recognize this desktop as the one used by that operating system.

Icons

The taskbar

On the desktop shown on the previous page is a window that displays a tip. Also visible are *icons* that represent some of NT's most commonly used tools. Running horizontally across the bottom of the screen is the *taskbar*, which has a Start button at one end and a clock at the other. The icons and taskbar are the primary items you'll use to get your NT work done, and you'll learn all about them in this book.

The mouse pointer

Floating somewhere on the desktop is the *pointer*, which is electronically connected to your mouse. The mouse is essential equipment for working with NT and the application programs you use. As you move the mouse, the pointer moves correspondingly on the screen, allowing you to point to the item you want to work with. The pointer is often an arrow, but it can take other forms, such as an I-beam when over text or an hourglass when NT or a program is processing information. When the pointer is where you want it, you click one of the mouse buttons to activate the item under it, choose a command, and so on, or you double-click to give other types of instructions, as follows:

No taskbar?

If the taskbar is nowhere in sight, you can display it temporarily by pointing to the thin border at the bottom of your screen. The taskbar disappears again when you move the pointer. To make the taskbar hang around a bit longer, you can press Ctrl+Esc to make the taskbar appear with the Start menu open, and then press Esc to close the Start menu. The taskbar disappears again if you click the desktop. To display the taskbar permanently, see page 180. If the taskbar is not at the bottom of the screen but instead rests against one of the other three edges, you can leave it where it is and still follow along with our examples. Or you can move it by pointing to it, holding down the mouse button, dragging it to the bottom of the screen, and releasing the mouse button (see page 178).

• **Clicking.** Clicking is simply a matter of pressing and releasing the primary mouse button once. In this book, we assume that you are using the left mouse button as your primary button and your right mouse button as your secondary button. So when we say *Click the Recycle Bin*, we mean *Move the pointer over the Recycle Bin and click the left mouse button*. If you have reversed the primary and secondary buttons, you would click the right mouse button instead. (We describe how to reverse the buttons on page 191.)

- **Right-clicking.** You perform this action by pressing and releasing the secondary mouse button once. When we say *Right-click the desktop*, we mean *Move the pointer to a blank area of the desktop and click the right mouse button.* If you have reversed the buttons, you would click the left mouse button instead.

- **Double-clicking.** To double-click, you quickly click the primary (usually left) mouse button twice. (If you have trouble double-clicking, see page 191 for information about how to adjust NT's response to your double-click speed.)

Before we can explore the desktop, we need to deal with the Welcome window. (If you don't see a Welcome window on your screen, read the following paragraphs but skip the instructions.) You will do almost all of your work with NT in some sort of *window* (a rectangle with a *title bar* across the top that describes the function of the window or shows the name of the program and document displayed in it). In this case, the window displays some tidbit of information about NT. (Clicking What's New displays an overview of improvements to the operating system. Clicking Help Contents enables you to find information about a specific feature, and clicking Next Tip displays a different tip.)

Windows

At the right end of the Welcome window's title bar is a Close button designated with an X. You can either click this button or click the Close button in the bottom right corner of the window to close the Welcome window. Follow these steps:

1. First, move the mouse so that the pointer is over the check box in the bottom left corner of the Welcome window and click the box to remove the check mark, which deselects the option. That way, you won't see this window every time you turn on your computer.

2. Click the Close button at the right end of the title bar to close the window.

The Close button

We'll talk more about windows in a moment, and about check boxes and buttons in Chapter 2. Now, let's explore the desktop.

Working with Icons

The icons on your desktop represent elements of NT that we will cover later in the book. As you install application programs on your computer, those programs may add icons to the desktop, to the point where your efficiency may suffer because of the clutter. You need to know how to manipulate icons to keep your desktop neat and tidy. Try this:

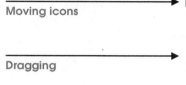

Moving icons

Dragging

1. Point to the Inbox icon, hold down the left mouse button, move the pointer to the top right corner of the desktop, and release the button. This hold-move-release action is called *dragging*. As you move the pointer, a shadow image of the Inbox icon moves with it, and when you release the mouse button, the icon jumps to its new location.

2. Repeat step 1 to move the Internet Explorer and My Briefcase icons below the Inbox icon.

3. Drag the Recycle Bin icon upward to fill the space below the Network Neighborhood icon. Your screen now looks something like this:

4. If you have any other icons on your desktop, move them to the bottom right corner of the screen.

You don't have to worry about aligning your icons precisely, but if tidiness is important to you, follow these steps to nudge your icons into straight lines:

1. Right-click an empty area of the desktop. Remember, this means click the secondary (usually right) mouse button once. You see this list, which is called an *object menu*:

Aligning icons

Object menus

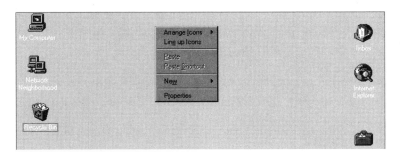

An object menu like this one appears whenever you right-click an object. The menu provides easy access to the commands that perform actions commonly associated with the object. (We talk more about menus and commands on page 35; for now, simply follow along.)

2. Point to Line Up Icons and click the left mouse button. NT straightens up the icons in their separate areas on the desktop.

Suppose you don't like icons scattered in the corners of the screen after all. You can tell NT to rearrange them, like this:

1. Right-click the desktop and point to Arrange Icons. NT displays a submenu like this one:

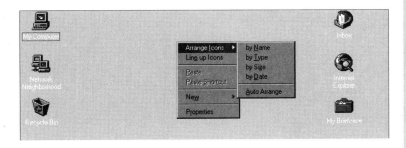

2. Point to By Name and click. NT realigns all the icons on the left side of the desktop.

Icon spacing

You can control the horizontal and vertical space between icons by clicking the Start button, pointing to Settings, clicking Control Panel, and double-clicking the Display icon. Then click the Appearance tab, click the arrow to the right of the Item box, and select either Icon Spacing (Horizontal) or Icon Spacing (Vertical). In the adjacent Size box, use the arrows to increase or decrease the number of pixels between icons. (Pixels are the small dots used to create images on the screen.)

If you want NT to act like a drill sargeant and automatically straighten up your ranks of icons, this is what you do:

Auto-arranging icons ▶

1. Right-click the desktop, point to Arrange Icons, point to AutoArrange, and then click. Nothing seems to happen, but behind the scenes, NT is now on duty.

2. Drag the Inbox to the middle of the desktop. When you release the mouse button, the remaining icons move up to fill the Inbox's place, and the Inbox icon snaps back to the left side of the desktop, but at the bottom of the rank.

3. Right-click the desktop, point to Arrange Icons, point to By Name, and click. The default pecking order is restored.

4. Right-click, point to Arrange Icons, point to AutoArrange, and click to send NT off-duty. Now you can move the icons wherever you want them.

Being able to shuffle icons on your screen is all well and good, but why are they there? Icons are not just cute little pictures; they represent programs and other computer elements, such as hardware, storage areas, or documents. Double-clicking an icon carries out a specific action, such as starting its program or displaying its contents. Here's an example:

The Recycle Bin icon ▶

1. Double-click the Recycle Bin icon. This window opens:

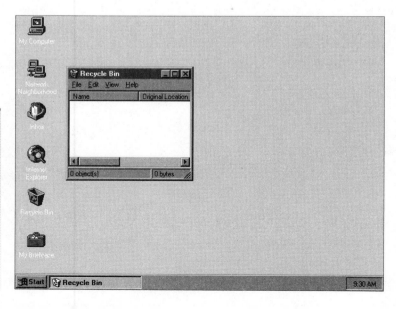

Why aren't the icons in alphabetical order?

If you choose Arrange Icons and then By Name to arrange the icons on your desktop, you may wonder why NT doesn't put them in alphabetical order. The icons NT creates are moved to their default locations. Any icons you add will be arranged alphabetically.

The Recycle Bin is an area on your hard drive to which files are moved when you "delete" them. Our Recycle Bin is currently empty, but yours may contain deleted items. (See page 87 for information about how to use the Recycle Bin.)

2. Notice that a button representing the Recycle Bin window has appeared on the taskbar at the bottom of the screen. We'll talk more about this button in a moment.

Leave the Recycle Bin window open for now and watch what happens to it as you work your way through the next section.

Working with the Start Button

An important feature of the desktop is the Start button at the left end of the taskbar. As its name implies, you can start many tasks by clicking this button. Follow these steps:

1. Move the pointer to the Start button at the left end of the taskbar at the bottom of the screen, and click the left mouse button once to display this Start menu:

The Start button

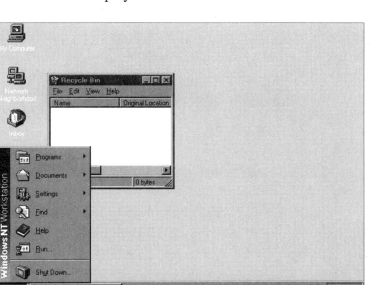

A *menu* is simply a list of items. In this case, the items are shortcut ways of carrying out common tasks, such as starting programs, finding and opening files, changing system settings, and getting information.

Start menu variations

Your Start menu may look different from the one we show, depending on what programs are installed on your computer and whether your Start menu has been customized. See page 120 for information about how to add items to the Start menu.

2. Move the pointer to Settings but don't click. NT displays this *submenu* of items:

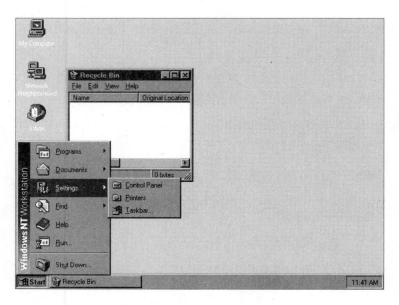

3. Move the pointer to Control Panel and click. Your desktop now looks like this:

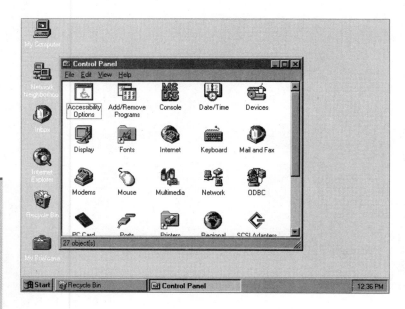

A full taskbar

If you open many windows, the taskbar can get pretty full of buttons. NT then abbreviates the button names to accommodate them all. If you can't tell which window a button represents, point to the button for a brief moment, and the full window name will pop up.

The Control Panel window contains a bunch of icons representing programs that control various aspects of your computer system. (You may have fewer, more, or different icons, depending on your system setup.) We won't explore these icons here; we'll save that discussion for Chapter 7.

The Control Panel

Notice that you didn't have to close the Recycle Bin window before opening the Control Panel window. Although the Control Panel window completely obscures the Recycle Bin window, the Recycle Bin is still open, as indicated by its button on the taskbar.

Window Basics

As the name *Windows NT* implies, when you're working with NT or one of its programs, you're always working in a window. So while we have these two windows open, it makes sense to learn some basic windowing skills before we go any further. (By the way, the *NT* part of the name seems to be a holdover from the first version of the operating system, which we have heard was touted as *New Technology*.)

Sizing and Moving Windows

With many programs, you'll want to work in a window that occupies the entire screen so that you can see as much of a document as possible. Sometimes, however, you'll want the window to take up less of the screen so that you can see other items on your desktop. Two buttons clustered with the Close button at the right end of the title bars of most windows allow you to quickly contract and expand the windows. You can also size the windows manually. Try this:

1. Point to the Control Panel window's title bar. Then move the pointer over the Maximize button (the middle of the three buttons at the right end of the title bar) and click. The window expands to fill the entire screen and the Restore button replaces the Maximize button on the title bar, as shown on the next page.

The Maximize button

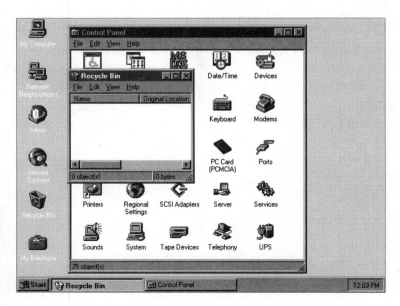

The Restore button

2. Click the Restore button. The window shrinks again, and the Maximize button replaces the Restore button.

Switching windows

3. Click the Recycle Bin button on the taskbar to bring its window to the forefront, like this:

Flipping between Restore and Maximize

When a window is maximized, you can restore it to its previous size by double-clicking its title bar. Double-clicking the title bar of a window that does not fill the entire screen maximizes the window.

Notice that the title bar of the active window is a brighter color than that of the inactive window, and that its button on the taskbar is brighter and appears "pressed."

4. Click the Recycle Bin window's Maximize button to expand the window to fill the screen.

5. Click the Control Panel button on the taskbar to make it the active window.

Except for the windows of some very simple programs, all windows that don't occupy the entire screen have *frames*, and most frames can stretch and shrink to make their windows larger or smaller. As you move the pointer over different parts of a frame that is resizable, the pointer becomes a two-headed arrow, indicating the directions in which you can move the frame to change its size. You can move the sides of the window frame to the left and right, move the top and bottom of the frame up and down, and move the corners up and down diagonally. Let's experiment:

◀── Frames

1. Point to the left side of the window frame and when the pointer changes to a double-headed arrow, hold down the left mouse button, move the mouse to the left to make the window wider, and release the mouse button.

◀── Sizing manually

2. Point to the bottom of the frame and drag up until the window is about 2 inches tall. Because the window is no longer big enough to display all its contents, a scroll bar appears down the right side. Don't worry about this for now; we talk about scrolling on page 39.

3. Point to the Resize box in the bottom right corner of the window and drag in any direction to change the window's height and width simultaneously. (Not all windows have a Resize box, but if the pointer changes to a two-headed arrow over their frames, you can drag to size them.)

◀── The Resize box

4. Point to the window's title bar and drag to the right or left. The entire window moves to its new location. (You can also move a window with the keyboard; see the tip on page 34.)

◀── Moving windows

5. Now click the Maximize button on the title bar to expand the window so that it fills the screen. The Maximize button is replaced by the Restore button, and the window's frame disappears. (Because a maximized window doesn't have a frame, you can't manually resize it.)

You can shrink the window to its minimum size and tuck it out of sight under its button on the taskbar. Although it's not visible, a minimized window is still accessible, as you'll see if you follow these steps:

The Minimize button

1. Click the Minimize button (the left button of the three at the right end of the title bar). The window appears to shrink into its button on the taskbar, the button turns gray to indicate that its window is inactive, and the only other open window, the Recycle Bin, becomes active.

2. Redisplay the Control Panel window by clicking its button on the taskbar.

Arranging Windows

What if you want an unobstructed view of all open windows? You could take the time to size each window in turn, but here's an easier way:

1. Right-click a blank spot on the taskbar to display this object menu of commands associated with the taskbar:

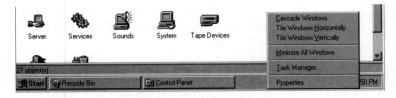

We discuss the Task Manager on page 111 and the Properties command on page 179. Here, we'll just play around with the first four commands.

Minimized windows are not arranged

If any open programs are minimized or if they have open dialog boxes, their windows are not included in screen rearrangements carried out using the four taskbar commands.

2. Click Tile Windows Horizontally. The result is shown on the facing page.

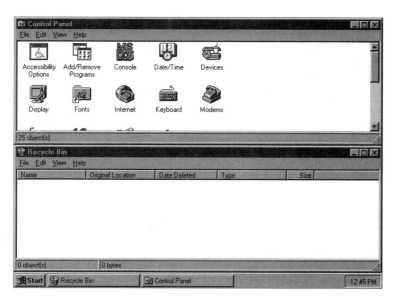

3. Right-click the taskbar and click Tile Windows Vertically to see that effect, and then right-click again and click Cascade Windows.

4. After you implement a window arrangement, a command that lets you undo that arrangement is added to the object menu. To see the effects of this command, right-click the taskbar and click Undo Cascade.

Undoing window arrangements

5. Finally, right-click and click Minimize All Windows to tuck both windows under their buttons on the taskbar.

Minimizing all windows

Getting Help

Using NT is fairly intuitive, and this book will help you find your way around so that, most of the time, you will know exactly what to do and how. However, for those times when you stumble, you'll want to consult NT's Help feature. Think of the Help feature as an encyclopedia-sized book in which you can look up just about any topic. NT provides Help topics for all its components, which you access like this:

1. Click the Start button, point to Help on the Start menu, and click to display the dialog box shown on the next page.

Help with programs

Most Windows programs have Help features that function pretty much the same as NT's. In a program, you can often press the F1 key to instantly access the Help dialog box.

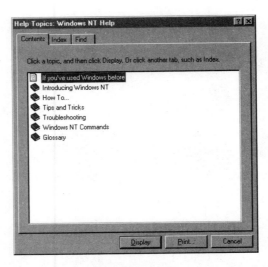

We don't go into detail about dialog boxes here (page 37 has the scoop). For now, just follow our steps. As you can see, the Help Topics dialog box is multilayered, with each layer designated by a tab like a file-folder tab. The Contents tab is currently displayed. (If it's not, click Contents.) This tab organizes help topics in broad categories.

Using the Contents tab

2. Double-click the book icon to the left of Introducing Windows NT to display a list of the available categories.

3. Double-click the book icon to the left of A List Of What's New to display a list of topics.

4. Double-click the question-mark icon to the left of A New Look And Feel to display this topic window:

Help's hidden information

In some topics, clicking a shortcut button (a small gray button with an arrow) takes you from the topic directly to the dialog box in which you can perform the task you are inquiring about. Clicking a small gray button without an arrow takes you to a related topic. Clicking a word underlined with dots displays a pop-up definition of that word.

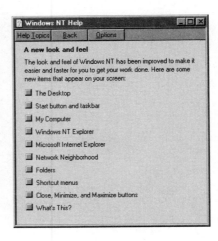

5. Click the box to the left of Start Button And Taskbar and read the information in the topic window.

6. Click the Close button at the right end of the active window's title bar, and then click the other window's Close button.

To search for specific information in Help, follow these steps:

1. Click the Start button, click Help, and click the Index tab to display this layer of the Help Topics dialog box:

Using the Index tab

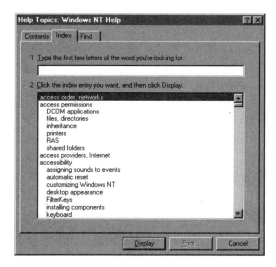

2. Type *shut* in the step 1 edit box. The list box below scrolls to the topics starting with those letters.

3. Click *shutdown, system* and click the Display button to see this list of related topics:

4. Click *To shut down your computer* and click Display to see the topic window shown on the next page.

Annotations

Choosing Annotate from Help's Options menu displays a text window in which you can add a note to the current help topic for future reference. When you click Save to close the window, a small paperclip icon appears next to the topic name. Just click the icon to display your note.

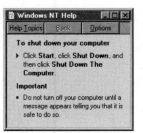

5. Click the window's Close button.

When you first start using NT, you'll probably want to stick to the Contents and Index tabs when looking for information. But once you feel more comfortable working with dialog boxes, you might want to try using the Find tab, which searches through the text of the topics instead of relying on topic headings. Before you can use this method of searching, you must use the Find Setup Wizard, which appears when you click the Find tab for the first time, to create a list of all the words in the topics. Thereafter, clicking the Find tab displays a dialog box in which you enter the word(s) for the topic you want to find, select matching words to narrow your search, and then select a topic and click Display.

Using the Find tab

Whichever method you use to find the information you need, once the topic is displayed, you can click the Options button at the top of the topic window and choose a command—for example, to annotate the topic with your own comments (see the tip on the previous page) or to print it. You can click the Help Topics button to return to the Help Topics dialog box without closing the topic window, and if you have jumped around from topic to topic, you can click the Back button to retrace your way back to where you started.

You might want to explore NT's Help feature on your own for a while. When you've finished, rejoin us as we take you through the steps for turning off your computer.

When you need advice

The support provided by Microsoft for Windows NT is different from that provided for its application programs. Comprehensive support is available for contracting organizations; check with your network administrator. If your organization has not contracted for support, you can get answers to common questions via fax by calling (800) 936-4400, or you can check the Microsoft Knowledge Base on The Microsoft Network (MSN) and other online services, and on the Internet at *www.microsoft.com*. You can also tell your troubles to a real live person, but only once. Call (425) 635-7018 and have your product identification number handy.

Shutting Down Your Computer

Well, this section is going to be easy, because you've already learned from NT's Help feature how to turn off your computer. A word of warning: never flip your computer's on/off switch without running through the shut-down procedure. NT does a lot of housekeeping at the end of each session to ensure that your computer will function properly the next time you turn it on. If you simply flip the switch, none of this housekeeping will get done, and there's no telling how future sessions might be affected. Here's how to shut down correctly:

← WARNING

1. Click the Start button and then click Shut Down. (It doesn't make sense to stop from the Start menu but you'll get used to it.) NT displays the Shut Down Windows dialog box:

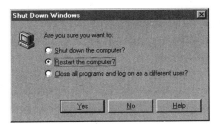

This dialog box contains a set of options that are fairly self-explanatory. (The last one applies only to computers that are on a network or have user profiles; see page 133.)

2. If necessary, click Shut Down The Computer to select it, and then click Yes. NT records information about this session, including the fact that the Recycle Bin and Control Panel windows are minimized on the taskbar, and then displays a message telling you that you can turn off your computer. (You can click the Restart button if you change your mind.)

3. Turn everything off.

Well, that's it for the quick tour. In the next chapter, we'll focus on finding and organizing documents.

Locking your computer

Suppose you want to stop using your computer for a while but not completely shut it down, and you want to prevent other people from using it while you are away. To lock your computer, press Ctrl+Alt+Delete. Then in the Windows NT Security dialog box, click the Lock Workstation button. To unlock the computer, press Ctrl+Alt+Delete again and enter your user name and password. To shut down your computer so that someone else can log on (the person working the next shift for example), click the Start button, click Shut Down, select the Close All Progams And Log On As A Different User option in the Shut Down Windows dialog box, and click Yes. You or another user can then press Ctrl+Alt+Delete to log on. (You can also click the Logoff button in the Windows NT Security dialog box.)

Using Programs

While using WordPad to create a document, we demonstrate how to start programs and choose commands using menus and toolbar buttons. We also discuss multitasking, and we briefly look at running MS-DOS programs.

Choose commands from menus or use toolbar buttons

Manipulate all program, folders, and document windows the same way

Recycle information by copying and pasting it between programs

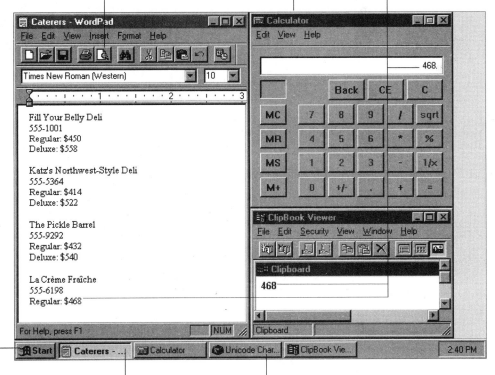

Start programs by choosing them from the Start menu

Switch among programs by clicking their taskbar buttons

Invisible but open programs are just a mouse click away

If you are like most computer users, you aren't interested in computers and their software for their own sakes. You want to do useful work. You want to send a letter, jot down notes for a meeting, draft a report, or analyze your income and expenses for the month. So the first thing you want to know about Windows NT Workstation 4 is how to start programs and create and save documents. By the time you finish this chapter, you'll have enough information to be able to use your own programs to carry out your daily tasks.

To get ready for the examples in this chapter, you need to be logged onto NT. If necessary, follow these steps:

1. Turn on your computer and select Windows NT Workstation Version 4.00 as your operating system.

2. Press Ctrl+Alt+Delete when instructed, and then log on.

   As you can see, NT remembers that the Recycle Bin and the Control Panel were open when you shut down your computer at the end of the previous chapter, and it displays their buttons on the taskbar. (NT does this for some of its own programs, but does not reopen applications like word processors or spreadsheets at startup unless they are listed on the Startup submenu; see page 125 for more information.)

Starting Programs

One of the simplest ways to get going is to start a program from the Start menu. (Some people use the terms *running*, *executing*, *launching*, and *loading* to mean starting a program. Generally, these terms can be used interchangeably.) Try this:

1. Click the Start button at the left end of the taskbar to display the Start menu shown on page 19.

2. Move the pointer to Programs but don't click. NT displays a submenu of programs preceded by unique icons and program groups preceded by folder icons. Clicking a program name starts that program and moving the pointer to a program group displays yet another submenu.

Adding/removing progams

We don't talk about adding and removing programs in this chapter. For a discussion of how to install or delete a program, see page 181, where we cover the tools in Control Panel.

3. Move the pointer to Accessories on the Programs submenu, but again, don't click. NT displays a submenu of all the programs that are part of the Accessories program group, and your screen now looks like this:

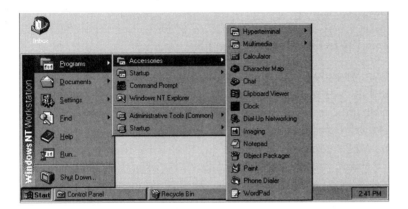

4. Move the pointer onto the Accessories submenu and then to WordPad, and click to start the WordPad program, a simple word processor that comes with NT. After NT starts Word-Pad, you see the window below on your screen. (Don't be alarmed if your window is a different shape or size; NT remembers the program window's previous appearance.)

Starting WordPad

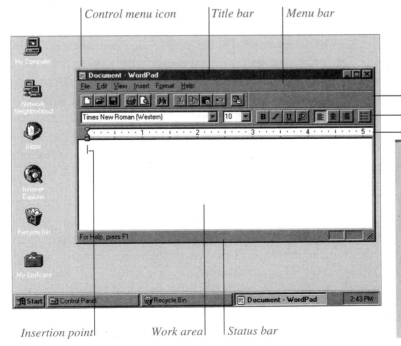

Programs submenu variations

The Programs submenu in our illustration is for a new computer on which no application programs have been installed. When you install a Windows program, the installation program may add an item or a group to the Programs submenu. You can also add items yourself (see page 121).

Notice that a button representing the WordPad window has been added to the taskbar.

Quitting from the taskbar →

5. Right-click the Recycle Bin button on the taskbar and then click Close in the object menu. Repeat this step for the Control Panel button.

6. Maximize the WordPad window.

Anatomy of a program window →

The window now on your screen has many of the characteristics of program windows. It has a title bar, which in this case tells you that the window contains a WordPad document. Below the title bar is a *menu bar*, which lists the command menus available for WordPad. Below the menu bar are two *toolbars*, which are collections of buttons that you can click to quickly carry out often-used commands. (We'll talk about the various ways of giving commands in a moment.) Below them is a *ruler*, a handy measuring tool that helps you design more complicated documents. At the bottom of the window is a *status bar*, where the program posts various items of useful information. Occupying the majority of the window is a *work area*, where you create your document. In this area, a blinking *insertion point* indicates where the next character you type will appear. (Don't confuse the insertion point with the pointer, which moves with your mouse and doesn't blink.)

Back to the title bar. At the left end is the *Control menu icon*. Clicking this icon displays a menu of commands for sizing and moving the window and quitting the program. (You can carry out these commands in other, simpler ways, so we won't cover this menu in detail; but you might want to read the adjacent tip.) At the right end of the title bar are the same Minimize, Maximize/Restore, and Close buttons you used in Chapter 1.

Moving windows with the keyboard

Sometimes a window can slide inexplicably so far off the screen that you can't grab its title bar and drag it back. If that happens, you can move the window by pressing Alt+Spacebar (the equivalent of clicking the Control menu icon), choosing Move from the Control menu, using the Arrow keys to bring the title bar into view, and pressing Enter.

The WordPad program is very simple and can handle only one document at a time. With more sophisticated programs, you can open two or more documents, in which case, each document is displayed in its own document window within the program window. Document windows have only title bars—no menu bars, toolbars, or status bars. Here's what the screen looks like when two documents are open in Word 97:

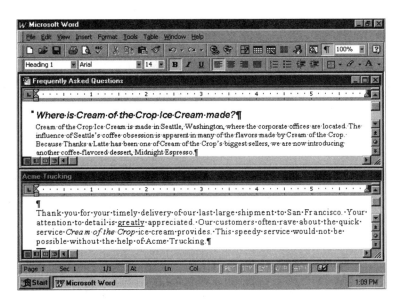

The program window's title bar now displays only the program name, and the document windows' title bars display the names of the documents the windows contain. On the taskbar, the program's button displays the name of the program. (Document windows don't get their own buttons.)

Command Basics

To get any useful work done, you have to be able to tell the computer what to do. NT and the Windows programs you run under NT provide a number of methods for giving instructions. We'll look at the primary methods in this section.

Choosing Commands from Menus

You've already seen the Start menu and know that it's just a list of tasks you might want to perform, including starting a program. Here, we'll look at a couple of other kinds of menus.

Using Menu-Bar Menus

In most Windows programs, you usually carry out tasks by choosing commands from the menus listed on the menu bar at the top of the program window. You click the name of the menu you want, and the menu drops down, displaying its list of commands. As part of the effort to give all Windows

Sizing and moving document windows

You can size a document window just like a regular window, except that a document window cannot be bigger than its program window. You can also move a document window around, but only within the frame of its program window. When you minimize a document window in some programs, the program puts a small title bar at the bottom of the program window. To redisplay the window, double-click the title bar.

Menu standardization ─────►

programs a common look, menus with commands that carry out similar tasks often have the same names and occupy the same position on the menu bar in different programs. The File menu and Help menu are examples of common menus. For example, the File menu usually contains commands such as New (for creating new items such as documents), Open (for opening existing documents), Save (for saving the current document), and Exit (for leaving the program). This menu always appears at the left end of the menu bar.

To choose a command from a menu, you simply click the command. To close a menu without choosing a command, you either click an empty spot away from the menu or press the Esc key. Let's take a look at a few menus and choose a command or two:

Dropping down a menu ─────►

1. Click the word *File* on the menu bar to drop down the File menu shown here:

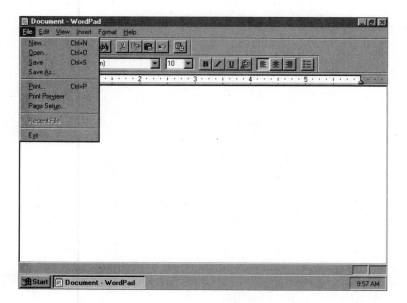

All Windows programs present their menu commands in consistent ways and use the following visual cues to tell you various things about the commands:

Help with commands

After dropping down a menu, you can point to a command to display a description of its function in the program's status bar.

• **Groups.** Commands that perform related tasks are grouped, and the group is separated from other commands by a line.

- **Unavailable commands.** Some commands are displayed in gray letters, indicating they are not currently available. For example, many programs have Cut and Copy commands on their Edit menus that appear in gray letters until the active document contains information that can be cut or copied.

- **Dialog boxes.** Some commands are followed by an ellipsis (...), indicating that you must supply information in a special kind of window called a dialog box before the command can be carried out. (More about dialog boxes in a moment.)

- **Keyboard shortcuts.** Key combinations are listed to the right of some commands, indicating that you can bypass the menu and carry out the command by pressing the corresponding keyboard shortcut.

- **Submenus.** Some command names are followed by a triangle, indicating that the command has a submenu. (You saw how submenus work when you started WordPad.)

- **Toggles.** Some commands are preceded by a check mark, indicating that you can "toggle" the command on and off.

    The commands on the File menu illustrate the first four visual cues in this list.

2. Now move the pointer over the word *View* on the menu bar to drop down that menu. (Notice that once one menu is open, you don't have to click to open another.)

3. Move the pointer down to the Ruler command—a toggle—and click. WordPad turns off the command and removes the ruler from the window.

4. Click View on the menu bar to display the View menu again, notice that the Ruler command is no longer preceded by a check mark, and then choose Ruler to turn on the command and redisplay the ruler.

Using Dialog Boxes

As you saw in Chapter 1, dialog boxes are NT's way of allowing you to give information or to select from several different options so that a particular command can be carried

Choosing commands with the keyboard

To use keyboard shortcuts to choose commands, you need to memorize the shortcuts. If you find it faster to use the keyboard but you don't want to tax your memory with key combinations, you can activate the menu bar by pressing Alt and then open the menu you want by pressing the underlined letter in the menu name. Next, choose a command by pressing the underlined letter in the command name. If you change your mind, press Esc to close a menu without choosing a command, and press Esc again to deactivate the menu bar. Once you learn the letters for menus and commands, you can type the key sequence quickly to choose the command. For example, to quit many programs, you can press Alt, then F, and then X.

out exactly the way you want it. To demonstrate further, let's create a memo:

1. Type *MEMO* and press Enter twice.

2. Type *To: All Staff*, press Enter, type *From: Julia*, press Enter, and then type *Date:* and a space.

Inserting the date

3. To insert the date, choose the Date And Time command from the Insert menu by clicking Insert on the menu bar to display that menu's list of commands (in this case, the objects that can be inserted in a WordPad document) and then clicking Date And Time. WordPad checks your computer for the current date and time and then displays the date and time in various formats in this dialog box:

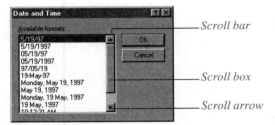

The dialog box is very simple and presents only one set of options, but as you saw when you explored NT's Help feature in the previous chapter, dialog boxes can be pretty complex, with options arranged on tabs. In this particular dialog box, you indicate the format you want for the date by selecting the format from a list box. The list of possible formats is too long to fit in its box, so a *scroll bar* appears down the right side, allowing you to scroll the list up and down to bring out-of-sight options into view. (See the tip on the facing page for more information about scroll bars.)

4. Click the arrowhead, called a *scroll arrow*, at the bottom of the scroll bar on the right side of the list box to see the other available date and time options.

Correcting mistakes

If you make a mistake while typing the memo, the simplest way to correct it is to press the Backspace key until you've erased the error and then retype the text correctly. If you need to move the insertion point to correct an error, point to the place in the existing text where you want the insertion point to appear and then click the left mouse button. Or you can use the Arrow keys to move the insertion point anywhere in the existing text.

5. Click the format that is the equivalent of May 19, 1997 to select it. NT indicates your selection by changing it to white type on a dark background, or *highlighting* it.

Selecting an option

6. Click OK. WordPad inserts the current date in the memo in the selected format.

7. Press Enter, and type *Subject: Directions to staff party.*

8. Press Enter three times and type the following note, pressing Enter where indicated:

As promised, here are directions to the Deer Creek Country Club. See you all there on July 4!

(Press Enter twice)

1. Take I-5 North to Alderfield. (Press Enter)
2. Take Exit 217 and turn right onto Deer Creek Road. (Press Enter)
3. Follow the road up-hill and down-dale for 7 miles, until you see Tiny's Trading Post on your left. (Press Enter)
4. Turn right onto Salish Road, and the entrance to Deer Creek Country Club is immediately on the left by the statue of grazing deer. (Press Enter)

When you finish typing, you see the results shown here:

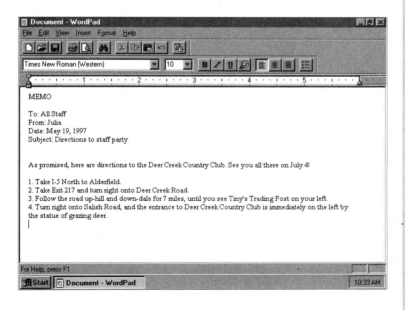

Scrolling

When a window is not big enough to display all of its contents, NT provides vertical and horizontal scroll bars so that you can bring other parts of the contents into view. You use the vertical scroll bar to move the contents up and down and the horizontal scroll bar to move the contents from side to side. Manipulating scroll bars is an important way of getting around in NT and Windows programs. You can use a couple of scrolling methods. Clicking the arrow at either end of a scroll bar moves the contents a line or a column at a time, whereas clicking on either side of the scroll box on the scroll bar moves the contents a "windowful" at a time. The position of the scroll box in relation to the scroll bar tells you where you are in the contents. For example, when the scroll box is in the middle of the scroll bar, the window is positioned roughly halfway through its contents. The size of the scroll box tells you about how much of the contents you can see at one time. For example, if the scroll box is half the length of the scroll bar, you can see half the contents. You can make the width of the sidebar thin or fat by selecting Scrollbar in the Item box on the Appearance tab of the Display Properties dialog box (see page 190) and changing its setting.

Now let's save the document. In the process, you'll use a more complex dialog box to specify a filename for the document, specify where to store it, and create a folder to hold this and related documents. You'll also get an idea of how your computer's storage (the electronic equivalent of a filing cabinet) is structured. Follow these steps:

Saving documents ➤ 1. Choose the Save As command from the File menu. WordPad displays the Save As dialog box shown here:

Why do you have to save documents?

Your documents exist only in the computer's memory until you save them on a disk. Memory is temporary and can be erased deliberately by turning off your computer and accidentally by power surges and failures. Disk storage is more permanent and can be erased only by using specific commands or due to (fairly rare) drive failures. If all you want to do is type a letter, print it, and send it, you may not need to store an electronic file of the letter on your hard drive. However, you'll want to save the file if you need an electronic record of what the letter said for future reference, if you want to use that letter as the basis for another letter, or if composing the letter is taking a while and you don't want to have to start over in the event of a computer glitch. The hard drives of the world are full of trivial documents that will never again see the light of day and that are not critical to "who said what to whom and when" audit trails. Check with the powers that be concerning your company policy about what files need to be saved and for how long.

All NT dialog boxes request information in consistent ways and, like commands, use visual cues to let you know the kind of information they need and how you should give it. Here's a list of the most common dialog box components:

- **Edit boxes.** You enter variable information, such as a filename, by typing it in an edit box, represented in the Save As dialog box by the File Name box. If you want to replace an existing entry in an edit box, select the entry and overtype the old text with the new. (See the tip on page 45 for information about selecting.)

- **Spinners.** If an edit box can contain only a number, it sometimes has a pair of up and down arrowheads, called spinners, at its right end. You change the entry either by selecting the existing number and typing a new one or by clicking one of the arrowheads to increase or decrease the number.

- **Sliders.** Number settings can also be represented by the position of a slider on a horizontal or vertical bar. To change the setting, you drag the slider.

- **List boxes.** When you need to select from several options, the options are often displayed in list boxes, and as you saw earlier, when more choices are available than can fit in the list box, the list box has a scroll bar. The list box we used earlier in the Date And Time dialog box presented a vertical list of options with a vertical scroll bar. In the Save As dialog box, icons accompany the options and there is no scroll bar. Regardless of the format of a list box, you select a listed option by clicking it. The option is then highlighted in the list.

- **Drop-down list boxes.** For space reasons, options are sometimes displayed in drop-down list boxes. Initially, a drop-down list appears as a box containing an option. At the right end of the box is a down arrowhead that you can click to drop down a list of other available options. To select an option, you simply click it. That option then appears in the collapsed list box. The Save As Type option at the bottom of the Save As dialog box is an example of a drop-down list box.

- **Combo boxes.** Sometimes an edit box and a drop-down list box are combined to form a combo box. You can either type in the information needed or you can select it from a drop-down list.

- **Check boxes.** Some options are presented with check boxes (small squares) in front of them. (You saw a check box at the beginning of Chapter 1, in the Welcome window.) Clicking an empty check box selects the associated option; a ✔ appears in the box to indicate that the option is active, or turned on. Clicking the box again removes the ✔ to indicate that the option is inactive, or turned off. Check boxes operate independently of one another, so if a dialog box presents a group of check boxes, you can select none, one, or all of the options, as required for the task at hand.

- **Options buttons.** Other options are presented with option buttons (small circles). There are no option buttons in the dialog box now on your screen, but as you'll see later, these buttons always appear as a group of mutually exclusive options. When you click an option button, a • appears in the button to indicate that the option is active. Because only one

Using the keyboard with dialog boxes

In some dialog boxes that require you to type information in edit boxes, it is often quicker to move around the dialog box using the keyboard than to constantly be switching between the keyboard and the mouse. You can move among the elements of a dialog box by pressing the Tab key. (If an edit box is active, it contains a blinking insertion point or a highlighted entry. Otherwise, the active element is designated by a dotted box.) With a list box or a group of option buttons, pressing Tab takes you to the active option. You can then press the Arrow keys to move through the options one at a time, press Home or End to move to the first or last option, or press Page Up or Page Down to display the previous or next boxful of options. When the option you want is selected, press Tab to move to the next element. No matter which element is active, pressing Enter immediately implements the command button that is surrounded by a heavy border. (If a command button is active, you can also implement it by pressing the Spacebar.) You can press the Esc key at any time to implement the Cancel button.

option in the group can be active at a time, the • disappears from the button of the previously active option.

- **Command buttons.** Most dialog boxes have at least two command buttons: one that closes the dialog box and carries out the command and another one that closes the dialog box and cancels the command. Some dialog boxes have additional command buttons, which you can use to refine the original command. As with commands on menus, if the label on a button is followed by an ellipsis (...), clicking the button opens another dialog box. One command button (in this case, Save) usually has a heavy border around it to indicate that you can press Enter at any time to implement that button.

- **Toolbar buttons.** Some dialog boxes have toolbar buttons that let you interrupt the current task and carry out a different one, or modify the current task in some way. The four buttons to the right of the Save In box are examples of this type of button.

In the Save As dialog box now on your screen, WordPad suggests *Document* as the name of the document in the File Name edit box. The Save In option at the top of the dialog box indicates that WordPad will save your document on the desktop unless you specify otherwise, and the list box below gives information about the components of the desktop. Take our word for it: saving a document with a generic name and saving it on the desktop are both bad practices (see page 76). Instead, you want to give the document a unique descriptive name and tuck it in a predictable location with other related documents so that it will be easy to find weeks or even months from now. Follow these steps:

Name conventions

Filenames and folder names cannot have more than 255 characters, and they cannot contain these characters:

: * | \ < > " ? /

See page 76 for more advice about naming files and folders.

1. The word *Document* is selected in the File Name box, so simply type *Directions* to replace it. (You can enter information in an edit box only if a blinking insertion point or a highlighted entry tells you the box is active.)

2. Click the arrow to the right of the Save In Box to drop down the hierarchical list of potential storage locations, as shown on the facing page.

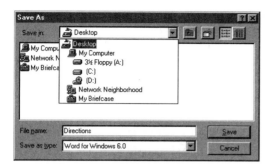

The desktop has these storage locations: My Computer (your PC), Network Neighborhood (the PCs on any network to which you are connected), and My Briefcase (a special area used to update files that you work with on another computer, such as a laptop; see page 84). My Computer, in turn, has several storage locations, which, depending on your particular hardware configuration, might consist of floppy drives, hard drives, and CD-ROM drives. If you are connected to a network, Network Neighborhood might have several storage locations as well, depending on which other computers are available to you. (We talk more about storage on page 62.)

Storage locations

3. Click (C:), which designates your computer's main hard drive. (C:) replaces Desktop in the Save In box, and the list box below it changes to display a set of folders in which various files are already stored on your C drive. (Your list will look different from the one shown in our illustrations because it reflects the folders and files on your C drive.)

You could save the memo directly on your C drive, but it's not a good idea. You wouldn't throw all your paper documents in one big pile if you expected to be able to easily find a specific document later. Instead, you'd organize the documents into categories and store them in file folders or something similar. Likewise, you need to somehow organize your computer documents for easy retrieval.

4. Click the Create New Folder button at the top of the dialog box to create a new folder on your C drive, as shown on the next page.

The Create New Folder button

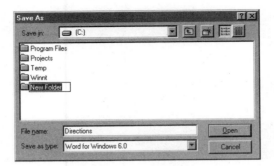

5. The title of the new folder is highlighted to indicate that it is selected. Type *Staff Party* to replace the selected title with a more descriptive one, and press Enter.

Opening a folder

6. Now double-click the folder icon to the left of Staff Party to open the folder. Staff Party replaces (C:) in the Save In edit box, and the list box is now empty because nothing is stored in the new folder yet.

Selecting a format

7. Click the down arrow to the right of the Save As Type option and select Rich Text Format (RTF) from the drop-down list.

8. Click the Save command button to save the memo in Rich Text Format in the Staff Party folder with the name Directions. The dialog box closes, and you return to the WordPad window, where Directions has replaced Document in the title bar and on the taskbar button.

Rich Text Format

By saving a document as a Rich Text Format (RTF) file, you ensure that you can open the document with its formatting intact if you have a word processor other than WordPad on your computer. In an RTF file, the formatting is translated into codes that can be interpreted by most word processors. Even if you open the file in your other word processor, saving it as an RTF file means that you will be able to open it in WordPad for examples later in the book.

Changing your mind

If you should change your mind about the settings that you have made in a dialog box but you can't remember what the settings were when you started, you can simply click Cancel or you can press Esc to close the dialog box. Then all of your changes are discarded and the previous settings remain in effect. You can then choose the command again and start all over if necessary.

Message boxes

All of the NT and Windows programs display message and warning boxes when a command you have chosen can't be carried out or there is a chance you might regret having chosen that command (for example, when deleting files). Clicking OK or Yes in such a message box not only acknowledges the message but also continues the command. On the other hand, clicking Cancel or No both closes the message box and cancels the command.

Using Object Menus

Windows programs make extensive use of object menus. As you have seen, these menus group together the commands you are most likely to use with a particular object. An object can be anything from an icon on the desktop to a toolbar in a program window to a word in a document. Try this:

1. Choose the Select All command from the Edit menu to select the entire memo.

Selecting the entire document

2. Move the pointer over the selection and click the right mouse button to display this object menu, which includes commands for manipulating the selected text:

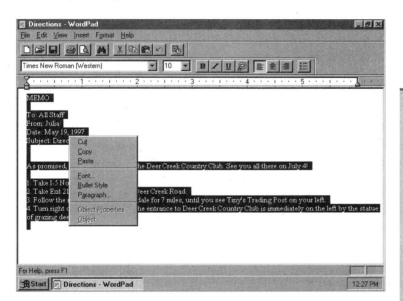

3. Choose Paragraph to display this dialog box:

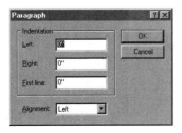

Selecting text

With NT and Windows programs, you can use standard techniques for selecting text. (Some programs add a few methods of their own, but we won't go into those here.) You can double-click a word to select it. You can point to the beginning of a block of text, hold down the left mouse button, and drag through the block, releasing the mouse button when the entire block is highlighted. You can click an insertion point at the beginning of a block, hold down the Shift key, point to the end of the block, and click to select all the words between the two clicks. (This action is sometimes called *Shift-clicking*.) Finally, you can click an insertion point, hold down the Shift key, and press the Arrow keys, releasing the Shift key when the text you want is highlighted.

4. Type *1* to replace the highlighted 0 in the Left edit box, and then click the OK command button. Here's the result:

Choosing Commands with Toolbar Buttons

Buttons vs. commands

Many Windows programs come with toolbars, which sport buttons and boxes that carry out common commands. Clicking a button carries out the corresponding command with its predefined, or default, settings. When you want something other than its default settings, you must choose the command from its menu. To familiarize yourself with the buttons on the WordPad toolbars, try this:

Using ToolTips

1. Point to each toolbar button in turn, pausing until the button's name appears in a box below the pointer.

2. Look at the status bar, where WordPad displays a brief description of the button you are pointing to.

You can use this helpful feature, which is called *ToolTips*, to identify the buttons in most Windows programs.

To demonstrate how to use toolbar buttons, we'll show you a very important button. The 1-inch left indent you just set looks a bit goofy. You could repeat the previous set of steps to reverse the Paragraph command, but here's an easier way:

1. Click the Undo button on the top toolbar (the equivalent of the Undo command on the Edit menu). WordPad resets the left indent to 0.

The Undo button

   Many Windows programs include an Undo feature, enabling you to reverse your last editing action. Knowing that you can always take a step backward makes experimenting less hazardous, so it's worth checking out the Undo feature of any program you use. (That way, you'll know exactly what to do if you paint yourself into a corner.) See the adjacent tip.

2. Move the pointer to the left of the word *MEMO* at the top of the document and when the pointer changes to a hollow arrow, click the left mouse button to select the entire line.

3. Click the Align Right button on the format bar (the second toolbar). The line jumps to the right side of the screen, and WordPad changes the look of the button on the format bar so that it appears "pressed." (Looking at the buttons on the format bar is a good way of telling at a glance what formatting is applied to selected text.)

The Align Right button

4. Click the Undo button to move the line back to the left side of the screen. Now the Align Left button appears pressed.

5. Click the Bold button on the format bar to make the text bold, and then click a blank area of the document to see this result:

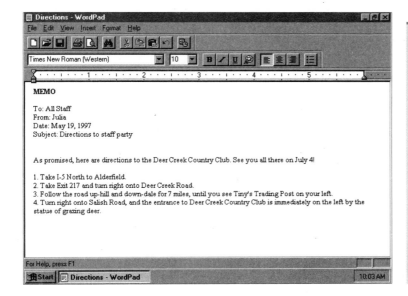

Undo variations

The Undo button can only remember a certain number of changes and can undo most, but not all, actions. Its capabilities vary from program to program, so experiment with less critical documents or save often so that you can backtrack. If Undo does not return your text to the desired formatting, you can always reselect it and apply the formatting manually using either buttons on the format bar or Format menu commands.

The Save button

6. Reselect MEMO and try clicking other buttons on the format bar and then clicking Undo. When you are ready, click the Save button to save the document with the current settings in the Save As dialog box, including the filename.

You might want to create a new document (see page 49) and practice selecting and formatting text using the buttons on the format bar. (See the tip about selecting on page 45.)

Multitasking

The term *multitasking* might sound intimidating, but the concept is simple: multitasking is carrying out two or more tasks at the same time. For example, you might be writing a report while your computer is printing another document, or your communications program is downloading information from an online service, or your e-mail program is receiving an incoming message. In practice, most people don't often take advantage of multitasking. They are more likely to open two or three programs and work with one while the others sit idly in memory, waiting until they are needed. The programs have been started and they are available, but they aren't actually doing any work.

Having several programs open at once saves you time by allowing you to keep all the information you need at your fingertips, whether it is stored in a report, a spreadsheet, a database, or any other type of document. If you're in the middle of writing a letter and need to look up some figures in a spreadsheet, you no longer have to stop what you are doing, quit the word processor, load the spreadsheet, find the figures, and then start your word processor again. You can simply flip between windows to get the information you need.

Foreground vs. background

Although you can have more than one program running at the same time, only one program can run *in the foreground*, meaning that its window is active and receiving input from you. Any other open programs run *in the background*, meaning that they are behind the scenes, either carrying out some prescribed task or waiting for your next instruction. Let's use the keyboard to start another program, and then we'll experiment:

1. Press Ctrl+Esc to open the Start menu, press the Up Arrow key until Programs is selected, and then press Enter. The Programs submenu opens with Accessories selected.

Starting Calculator

2. Press Enter to open the Accessories submenu, press the Down Arrow key until Calculator is selected, and press Enter to start NT's mini number cruncher:

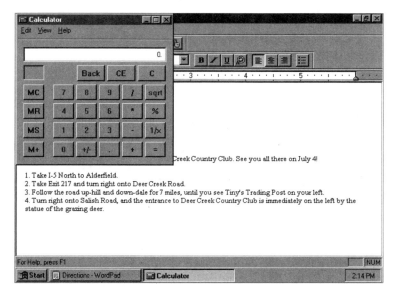

3. Click anywhere in the WordPad window to bring it to the foreground and make it active.

4. Click the New button and when WordPad asks you to specify a format for the new document, double-click Rich Text Document to both select that option and implement the default command button (the one with the heavy border).

The New button

Switching Among Running Programs

As you just saw, it's easy to switch to a program when you can see part of its window. If you are working in a maximized window and can't see the windows of programs running in the background, you can use the taskbar buttons to switch programs. As a demonstration, suppose you are responsible for providing appetizers for the staff party, and while browsing through the Yellow Pages, you use WordPad to take down information about potential caterers. Follow the steps on the next page.

Two identical buttons on the task bar?

If two identical program buttons are displayed on the taskbar, it means you have started the same program twice. Unless you have started them intentionally, you should close one of the copies to avoid confusion.

1. In the new WordPad document, type *Fill Your Belly Deli* and press Enter.

2. Type *555-1001*, and press Enter twice.

3. Add these delis to the list:

   Katz's Northwest-Style Deli
   555-5364 (Press Enter twice)

   The Pickle Barrel
   555-9292 (Press Enter)

The WordPad window looks like this:

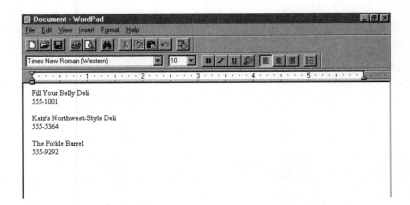

4. Now click the Save button to save the document. Because you haven't yet named the document, WordPad displays the Save As dialog box shown earlier on page 40. Next specify the Staff Party folder as the storage location and type *Caterers* as the filename. Then with Rich Text Format (RTF) selected as the Save As Type setting, click Save.

Suppose you are using your handy list to call the companies and get estimates. The first deli quotes you a per-person price of $6.25 for a regular assortment of appetizers and $7.75 for a deluxe assortment. You want to calculate the respective costs for 72 people. This is a job for Calculator:

1. Click the Calculator button on the taskbar to bring the Calculator window to the foreground.

More about Calculator

Calculator is capable of performing much more complex functions than those we describe here, and it provides several buttons you can use to store calculations. To find out the exact function of a particular button, as well as its keyboard shortcut, right-click it and choose What's This? from the object menu. To display a scientific calculator, choose Scientific from the View menu.

2. Click the buttons for 72, click *, click the buttons for 6.25, and click =. The display bar shows the total, 450.

3. Now you need to go back to the Caterers document to record the cost of the regular appetizers. Click the WordPad button on the taskbar to display its window. The Calculator window is once again obscured by the WordPad window.

4. Click at the beginning of the blank line after the first caterer's telephone number to position the insertion point there, type *Regular: $450*, and press Enter.

Here's another way to switch between open programs:

1. Hold down the Alt key and without releasing the key, press the Tab key. A window appears in the middle of the screen in which the open programs are represented by icons. A box indicates the program NT will switch to when you release Alt.

Using Alt+Tab

2. Still holding down the Alt key, press Tab again to move the box to the icon of the other program. Press Tab again and then release the Alt key. NT displays the Calculator window.

3. Click the C (for *clear*) button, click the buttons for 72, click *, click the buttons for 7.75, and then click =. The display bar shows the total, 558.

4. Use the Alt+Tab combination to switch back to WordPad, and with the insertion point at the beginning of the blank line after the regular cost, type *Deluxe: $558*, and press Enter.

Now suppose the second deli has quoted you a per-person price of $5.75 for a regular assortment of appetizers and $7.25 for a deluxe assortment. You have only a couple of programs open, so let's first arrange them so that you can see them both at the same time, and then enter the information:

1. Right-click a blank area of the taskbar and choose Tile Windows Vertically from the object menu to arrange the windows side-by-side.

2. Click the Calculator window's title bar to activate it, click C, click the buttons for 72, click *, click the buttons for 5.75, and click =. The display bar shows the total, 414.

3. Click the Caterers window, click an insertion point at the beginning of the blank line after the second caterer's telephone number, type *Regular: $414*, and press Enter.

4. Repeat steps 2 and 3 with the deluxe per-person amount to calculate the second caterer's deluxe cost and enter it in the document. Your screen looks like this:

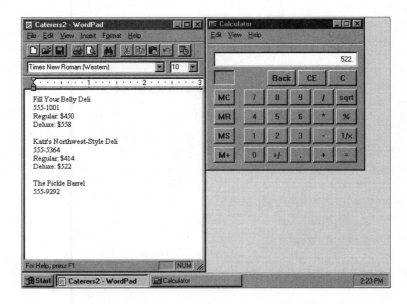

Sharing Information Among Programs

With Windows NT Workstation, it is easy to use the information from one program in another program. Need a logo for your letterhead? You can create one with a paint program, copy it to a storage area in memory called the *Clipboard*, and paste it into a word-processing document. Because NT allows you to run the paint program and the word-processing program simultaneously, moving from one program to the other is a simple matter of clicking the mouse button.

Let's experiment with transferring information using Word-Pad and Calculator. Follow these steps to complete the information for the third caterer:

1. Click the Calculator window, click C, click the buttons for 72, click *, click the 6 button, and click =. The display bar shows the regular appetizer cost at $6 per person, 432.

The Clipboard

The Clipboard is a temporary storage place in your computer's memory in which cut or copied data from all NT and Windows programs is stored. You can use it to transfer data within the same program or from one program to another. Each object you cut or copy overwrites the previous object. (See page 55 to watch this process in action.) Because the Clipboard is a temporary storage place, shutting down your computer erases any information you have stored there.

2. Choose Copy from the Calculator's Edit menu to copy the value in the display bar to the Clipboard.

Copying information

3. Click the Caterers window, click an insertion point at the beginning of the blank line after the third caterer's telephone number, and type *Regular:* followed by a space and *$*.

4. Choose Paste from WordPad's Edit menu to paste the total from the Calculator into the document. Then press Enter. (For consistency, you can delete the space WordPad inserts before the number.)

5. Repeat steps 1 through 4 to calculate the third caterer's deluxe cost at $7.50 per person and paste it into the document.

To give you more practice, we'll show you how to use Character Map, an NT program you can use to insert special characters in your documents. We're going to add an entry for a fourth deli called La Crème Fraîche (which means *Fresh Cream*) to the list. Follow these steps:

1. With the Caterers window active, click an insertion point at the beginning of the blank line below the third caterer, press Enter, and type *La Cr*.

2. Click the Start button, display the Programs and Accessories submenus, and click Character Map to display this window:

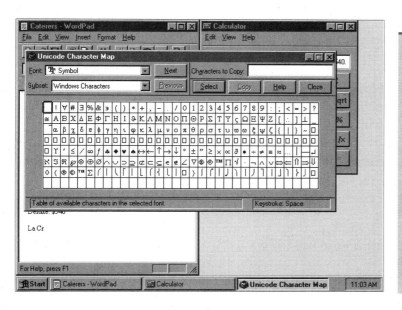

Entering characters with the keyboard

In the bottom right corner of the Character Map window is the shortcut for entering the selected character from the keyboard rather than by copying it from Character Map. For example, you can type the *è* character without switching to Character Map by holding down the Alt key and pressing 0, 2, 3, and 2 keys on your keyboard's numeric keypad. (You can't use the number keys across the top of your keyboard.)

As you can see, the program displays all the characters available in the font specified in the Font box.

3. Click the arrow at the right end of the Font box and select Times New Roman from the drop-down list. The characters in the grid below change to reflect those available in that font.

4. Check that the Characters To Copy box is empty (if it's not, double-click the existing entry and press the Delete key), click *è* in the last row, verify in the magnified box that it's the character you want, and click the Select button. The program enters *è* in the Characters To Copy box, and the window now looks like this:

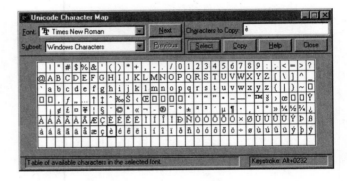

5. Click the Copy button to copy the character to the Clipboard.

The Paste button

6. Click the Caterers-WordPad button on the taskbar to activate the Caterers document and click the Paste button on the toolbar. The character appears at the insertion point.

The font size of *è* is 12 points, but the font size of the rest of the Caterers document is 10 points. Here's how to fix the problem:

What's a point?

Fonts are measured in terms of their height—the distance from the bottom of the descender characters in the font, such as *p*, to the top of the ascender characters, such as *h*. The unit of measure is called a *point* (abbreviated *pt*), and 1 point equals 1/72 inch.

1. Select *è* by dragging the mouse pointer over it so that it becomes highlighted. (If you have trouble selecting a single character with the mouse, point to the left of the line and click to select the entire line.)

2. Click the arrow at the right end of the Font Size box on the format bar to drop down a list of sizes, scroll upwards if necessary, and click 10.

Now let's complete the name of the fourth caterer:

1. Press the End key to move to the end of the line, type *me Fra*, and click the Unicode Character Map button on the taskbar to display its window.

2. Double-click the entry in the Characters To Copy box to select it, and press Delete.

3. Click î in the last row, click the Select button, click Copy, and then minimize Character Map to hide it on the taskbar.

4. Activate the WordPad window, click the Paste button to paste in the character, finish the name by typing *che* and pressing Enter, and then change the font size to 10 points.

5. On the next line, type *555-6198* as the telephone number and press Enter. Here are the results:

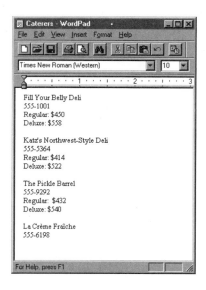

6. Click the Save button to save your work.

   The last item you copied, î, is still on the Clipboard and stays there until it is replaced by the next item you cut or copy, or until you quit NT. Let's sidetrack here to see the copied item on the Clipboard:

1. Click the Start button, display the Programs and Accessories submenus, and click Clipboard Viewer. NT starts ClipBook Viewer, which opens first a Clipboard window and then a Local Clipbook window in its work area.

   Starting ClipBook Viewer

2. Choose Clipboard from the Window menu to bring its window to the forefront, and then resize the ClipBook Viewer window so that it fits under the Calculator, like this:

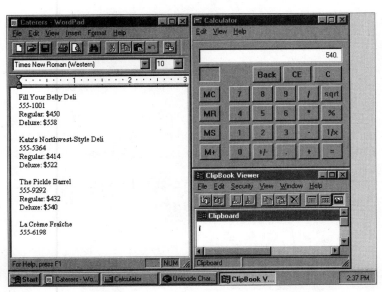

Clipbook Viewer

To save something you have cut or copied to the Clipboard for use at a later time, you can use Clipbook Viewer. Unlike the Clipboard, Clipbook Viewer can store several items. To save an item, first copy it. Then open Clipboard Viewer, which displays the Local Clipbook. (If necessary, you can select Local Clipbook from the Window menu.) Choose Paste from the Edit menu and enter a name for the item in the Paste dialog box. If you want other network users to be able to access the item, select the Share Item Now option. Then click OK. If you have shared the item, NT displays the Share Clipbook Page dialog box in which you can set this resource's permissions. To access the item later, open the Local Clipbook and open the item by double-clicking it. You can then copy the item and paste it in another program as usual.

3. Calculate the cost of regular appetizers at $6.50 per person and copy and paste the result in the Caterers document, noticing that the copied item replaces the existing item in the Clipboard window, like this:

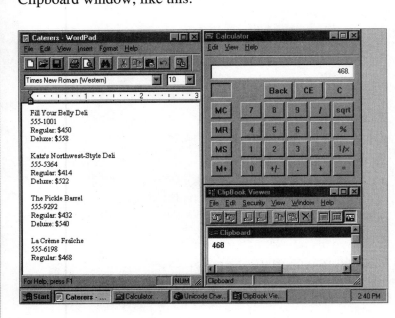

4. Repeat step 3 to calculate the cost of deluxe appetizers at $8 per person and paste the result in the Caterers document.

Once you have created a document, you'll often want to print it, but be patient. We discuss printing on page 107.

Quitting Programs

When you finish working with a program, you will probably want to close it before moving on to some other task. Closing a program—also called *quitting*, *leaving*, or *exiting* a program—couldn't be easier. On page 34, we quit a couple of programs from the taskbar. Here are a few more methods:

1. Click the Close button at the right end of the WordPad window's title bar. Because you have done some work since you last saved the document, WordPad displays this message box:

2. Click Yes to save the current version of Caterers and quit WordPad. The WordPad window closes and its button disappears from the taskbar.

3. Activate Calculator and instead of clicking its Close button, press Alt+F4.

4. With Clipbook Viewer active on the desktop, choose Exit from its File menu.

5. Click Character Map's button on the taskbar and click either the button labeled Close on the right side of the window or the Close button at the right end of the title bar.

Using MS-DOS and MS-DOS Programs

If you've been working with computers for a while, you may be comfortable using MS-DOS commands or have a favorite MS-DOS program that you want to use under Windows NT Workstation 4. You'll be happy to know that MS-DOS is still

Quitting a program that's crashed

To increase its reliability, NT assigns each program its own area of memory to run in. That way, if a program crashes, it usually doesn't bring down the entire system. You can often close the misbehaving program and carry on working. To close the program, right-click the taskbar, choose Task Manager, and click the Applications tab. Or press Ctrl+Alt+Delete and click the Task Manager button. Next, select the program and click End Task. Then close Windows NT Task Manager. You will lose any unsaved work in that program, but your other work should be unaffected. If this process doesn't work, other programs may have become unstable, and your best bet is to shut down and restart NT. The moral: save your work regularly to prevent mishaps from becoming tragedies.

available and that with NT, it is fairly easy to work with most MS-DOS programs. Let's experiment:

Starting Command Prompt →

1. Choose Command Prompt from the Programs submenu of the Start menu to load the NT version of MS-DOS. You see this window with the familiar C:\> prompt:

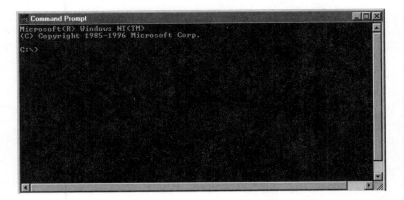

2. Press Alt+Enter to switch Command Prompt to full-screen mode. Command Prompt completely takes over the screen, emulating regular MS-DOS.

3. Type *mem* and press Enter. This MS-DOS command reports how much memory is available for MS-DOS programs.

4. Press Alt+Enter to switch back to windowed mode.

5. Type *edit* and press Enter to start the MS-DOS text editing program, which displays a window like this one:

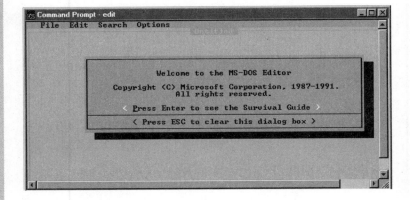

Customizing MS-DOS sessions

To change the color scheme of the MS-DOS screen, first start the program. Next, right-click the title bar and choose Properties from the object menu. Display the Colors tab and select the item whose color you want to change. Select a color from the row of boxes below. To fine-tune the colors, adjust the settings in the Selected Color Values section. Then click OK. When Windows displays the Apply Properties To Shortcut dialog box, select the option you want and click OK.

6. Press the Esc key to clear the screen, and because we are not going to actually do anything in MS-DOS Editor, choose Exit from the File menu to quit the program.

Quitting an MS-DOS program

7. At the C:\> prompt, quit Command Prompt by typing *exit* and pressing Enter.

Quitting Command Prompt

You can start an MS-DOS program without going through Command Prompt. Try this:

1. Choose Run from the Start menu to display the dialog box shown here, which you can use to start Windows programs as well as MS-DOS programs:

Using the Run command

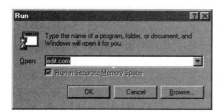

NT anticipates that you want to restart the MS-DOS Editor program and enters its name in the Open edit box.

2. Click OK to start the program and then repeat steps 6 and 7 above to quit the program and return to the NT desktop.

When you finish working with an MS-DOS program, you should quit the program just as you would when working in MS-DOS. It's tempting to simply click the Close button of a windowed program, but quitting in the usual way minimizes the risk of any problems. If you click the Close button of MS-DOS Editor, for example, NT displays a message box. You then have to click an End Task button to close the program. Similarly, if you try to shut down your computer with MS-DOS Editor still open, NT automatically closes open Windows programs but reminds you to manually close the editor.

In spite of these drawbacks, if you are an MS-DOS aficionado, a few extra clicks and key presses will be a small price to pay for the ability to run familiar old programs under your new operating system.

Paths

Some dialog boxes ask for the path of a document, which you can think of as the document's address. For documents stored on your computer, this address starts with the drive and traces through folders to the document, separating each storage level from the previous one with a backslash (\). For example, C:\Staff Party\Directions is the path of the Directions document stored in the Staff Party folder on your C drive. The path of a document stored on another computer on your network starts with the computer name, followed by the drive, any folders and subfolders, and the document's filename.

3

Working with
Your Computer's Resources

We track down and open existing documents using
My Computer, Windows NT Explorer, and the Find
command. Then we show you how to get organized
by creating folders and moving, copying, renaming,
and deleting documents.

Use My Computer to
visually manage your
folders and documents

Use Windows NT Explorer
to organize your folders and
documents in list format

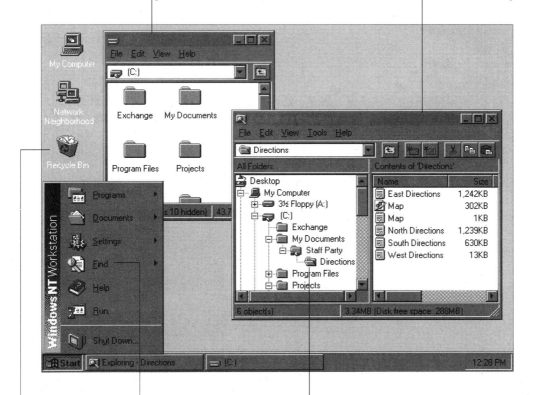

Remove unwanted
folders and
documents via
the Recycle Bin

Locate folders and
documents with the
Find command

Create new folders to
organize your documents
for easy retrieval

For some people, organizing computer files is a difficult chore. They'll start a program, open a new document, save it with a name like Letter, and think they'll be able to retrieve it without much trouble if they ever need it again. Because these people are busy, they often don't take the time to work out a file-naming system, and they may end up wasting a lot of time searching for a particular document. Is it Letter, or Smith Letter, or 6-12 Letter? And is it stored in the Letters folder, or the Smith folder, or the June folder?

With Windows NT Workstation 4, you no longer have to trust your memory to organize and retrieve documents efficiently. First, you can use up to 255 characters, including spaces, in a filename. So you can use filenames like Letter Written On 6-12-97 To Smith Associates About The Hunter Project to describe your documents. Second, NT provides two organizational aids, My Computer and Windows NT Explorer, that you can use to shuffle your documents into folders in any way that makes sense to you.

In this chapter, we first discuss some organizational concepts. Then we show you how to find and open documents. Finally, we look at organizational strategies and techniques that make locating your documents as easy as possible.

Storage Basics

When you saved documents in Chapter 2, you saw that your computer storage space is divided into logical groups. For simplicity, you might want to think of this division as taking place on five levels:

The desktop

- **Level One.** The *desktop*, the by-now familiar opening screen of NT, provides access to all the storage resources available to you while you are working. (The icon on the left represents the desktop from another window. While you are looking at the desktop, you won't see this icon.)

Local and network storage

- **Level Two.** The desktop displays a My Computer icon representing your computer's storage, which we'll refer to as *local storage*. It also displays a Network Neighborhood icon representing the storage of any other computers available if you are connected to a network, which we'll refer to as *network storage*. Also at this level are the Recycle Bin, which holds objects you have deleted from both local and network storage; and My Briefcase, which helps you coordinate the use of files on multiple computers. (For information about the Recycle Bin and My Briefcase, see pages 87 and 84.)

- **Level Three.** Your local storage is divided into chunks of space called *drives*, which are designated by unique, single letters. Most computers have one hard drive, called *C*, and one or two floppy drives, called *A* and *B*. If you have other drives, such as a CD-ROM drive, they are also assigned letters (*D*, *E*, and so on). If your computer is on a network, your network storage is divided into chunks of space on other computers, which are designated by the computers' names. The computers are further subdivided into drives designated by letters. Also at this level are three *system folders*: Control Panel, which stores tools for customizing the way you work with your computer (see page 178); Printers, which stores a setup tool and printer information (see page 101); and Dial-Up Networking, which you use with a modem to access computers that are not on your network (see page 160).

- **Level Four.** Divisions within drives are called *folders*. Some folders have *subfolders* within them. (In this book, we use the term *folder* to mean any folder, designating folders within folders as *subfolders* only when the relationship is important.)

- **Level Five.** The lowest level is *files*, which are divided into two main categories: program files and data files. *Program files* contain instructions to the computer to run programs, such as a word processor or a graphics program, and they are written by programmers. Data files are the documents you create while running a program, such as a letter written using a word processor, or a picture drawn with a graphics program.

For example, you might write a report called *2nd Qtr Sales* and store it in a folder called *1997*. This folder is a subfolder of a folder called *Reports*, which is in turn a subfolder of a folder called *My Documents*, which is stored on the *C* drive of your computer. Your computer is the *local storage* component of all the resources available from your desktop. If

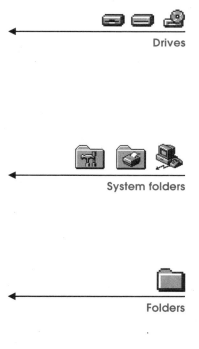

Drives

System folders

Folders

What does the little hand mean?

Some drive, folder, and file icons might be sitting in the palm of a little hand. These storage areas and files are "shared," meaning that they can be accessed by people other than the "owner" of the computer on which they are stored. Just because an object is shared doesn't mean that you can access it, however; you must have permission to use that object in order to use it. See page 93 for more information.

your computer's name is SALES1, the path of the document is *SALES1\C:\My Documents\Reports\1997\2nd Qtr Sales* (see the tip on page 59 for information about paths).

Bear in mind these levels of storage as we move on to explore ways of finding and organizing documents.

Opening Recently Used Files

When you want to open a document that you worked on fairly recently, you don't have to know where you stored it. For example, in Chapter 2, you used WordPad to create a document called Directions. Suppose you now want to change some of the instructions in the document. Follow these steps to open it and make the changes:

Opening a document from the Documents submenu

1. Click the Start button to open the Start menu and then point to Documents. NT displays a submenu of the documents you have worked on recently, as shown here:

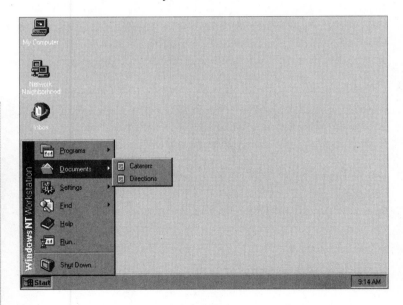

Clearing the Documents submenu

Sometimes you might want to start an NT session with an empty Documents submenu to avoid the clutter of old documents you don't need. To clear the submenu, right-click a blank area of the taskbar and choose Properties from the taskbar's object menu to display the Taskbar Properties dialog box, which has two tabs. Click the Start Menu Programs tab, click the Clear button in the Documents Menu section to remove the list of documents from the submenu, and then click OK to close the dialog box.

Programs can record up to 15 documents on this submenu. (Not all programs take advantage of this feature.) Once the submenu is full, older document records are deleted as new ones are added.

2. Click Directions. NT opens the document in its associated program so that you can begin editing.

Notice that you don't have to first start a program and then open the document. NT knows which program is associated with the document and starts that program automatically. (If you have Microsoft Word installed on your computer, NT starts Word instead of WordPad because it assumes you want to use the more sophisticated word processor. Don't worry, our steps will work with whichever program NT starts.)

Now let's change the memo and save it with a different name so that we will have a couple of documents to play with:

1. In the first instruction, change the word *North* to *South*. (Double-click *North* to select the word, and then type *South*.)

2. In the second instruction, change the word *right* to *left*.

3. Choose Save As from the File menu to display the dialog box shown earlier on page 40, press the End key to move the insertion point to the end of the File Name edit box's entry, press the Spacebar, and type *From North*. Leave all the other settings as they are and click Save to save this new version of the document with a different name.

4. Click the Start button and point to Documents to display its submenu, which now includes Directions From North as well as the original Directions. (Notice that you don't have to close or minimize the document window in order to access the Start menu and do other types of work.)

5. Click anywhere away from the menu to close it.

6. Now click the Close button to close the Directions From North window and quit the program in preparation for the next section.

Finding Files

You've just seen how to open a document you have recently worked on. But what if you need to retrieve a document that you worked on a while ago? If you know in which folder and on which drive the file is stored you can use My Computer or Windows NT Explorer, two programs that come with NT, to locate and open it. If you're hazy about the name of the

How does NT know which program to start?

When you save a file, NT adds an extension to the filename to identify the file type (see page 130 for information about extensions.) File types are associated with programs. For example, if you double-click a file with an xls extension, NT knows to open the file in Excel because the xls file type is associated with Excel. However, associations can change as you install new programs on your computer. For example, the rtf extension is associated with WordPad unless you install Word, which then takes over the association. To view or edit the associations, choose Options from the View menu and display the File Types tab (see page 130 for more information).

document or its location, you can use the Find command to track it down. We'll try finding a document stored on your own computer using all of these methods in the next three sections. In Chapter 4, we'll locate a document stored on a network computer by using another NT tool, Network Neighborhood (see page 98). As you'll see, you can also use these techniques to find and start programs.

Using My Computer

My Computer is represented by an icon directly on the desktop because it is frequently used for basic file management on your own machine. My Computer uses hierarchical windows to show you the structure of your local storage so that you can find the documents you need. The quickest way to become familiar with My Computer is to start using it, so follow these steps to find the Directions document, which is stored in the Staff Party folder on your C drive:

The My Computer icon

1. Double-click the My Computer icon to display this folder window:

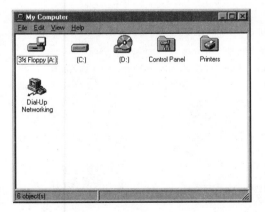

Notice that the window's button appears on the taskbar. (Don't worry if your window looks a bit different from ours. Your window contains icons representing the configuration of your particular computer, and some of your icons may have different names.)

2. Double-click the icon for your C drive to open its folder window and add its button to the taskbar.

Finding My Computer

If you have several windows open on the desktop, or if a window is maximized, the My Computer icon may be hidden. To find it, simply move or minimize the open windows.

3. Find the icon for the Staff Party folder (you may have to scroll the window) and double-click it to open its window and add its button to the taskbar. Three open folder windows are now stacked on your screen, which looks something like this:

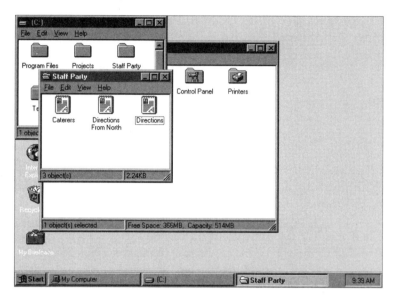

Notice that the title bar of the active Staff Party window is a different color than those of the windows beneath it.

Having located the document, let's see how to open it:

1. Double-click the Directions icon to both start the associated program and open the document. (See page 130 for information about associating programs.)

Opening a document from My Computer

To click or double-click?

Are you confused about when to click and when to double-click? The general rule is to click when you want to select something and to double-click when you want to carry out an action. If you have difficulty remembering that distinction, you can always click and wait to see if that accomplishes your goal. If it doesn't, double-click.

Shortcuts to folders

If you regularly use My Computer to move to the same folder, you might want to create a shortcut specifically for that folder. You can then save some time by simply double-clicking the shortcut to jump directly to the desired folder. For more information about how to create shortcuts, see page 116.

One folder window

Viewing each storage area in its own folder window can clutter the screen. To display all areas in the same window, choose the Options command from a folder window's View menu, click the bottom option button on the Folder tab, and click OK. Each area you open from then on is displayed in the active window. To move back one level, press Backspace.

2. Use the Save As command to save a copy of the document with the name *Directions From South*. (Before you click the Save button, be sure the Save As Type setting is still Rich Text Format.)

3. Click the Close button to close the document and quit the program, but leave the My Computer folder windows open.

You've probably noticed that folder windows are very similar to program windows (see page 33), except that, by default, they don't have toolbars. You move, size, minimize, maximize, restore, and close folder windows the same way you do program windows, and you choose commands from their menus the same way, too. Try this:

1. With the Staff Party window still active, click its Minimize button to hide the window under its button on the taskbar.

2. Click the My Computer button on the taskbar to bring that window to the top of the stack and make it active.

Checking storage space ➤ 3. If necessary, click the (C:) icon in the window to select it, and then take a look at the status bar at the bottom of the My Computer window. The status bar reports the number of objects selected and the capacity and amount of free space on your C drive.

4. Minimize the My Computer window, leaving only the (C:) window open on the desktop.

5. Click an empty area of the window so that nothing is selected. The status bar of this window reports the number of objects (folders and files) in the window and the amount of space occupied by the files in the window:

Folder window toolbars

By default, toolbars are not displayed in folder windows. However, you can turn on the toolbar for the active window by choosing the Toolbar command from the View menu. (Other windows are not affected by this change.) Included on this toolbar are buttons that allow you to move up one level; reconfigure network settings; cut, copy, or paste folders and documents; undo a deletion; and change the display of the files in the window. (You may need to enlarge the window in order to view all of the buttons.)

The total storage space is for all the files in the window, including files hidden from view. (See the tip below.) It does not include any files stored in subfolders of the (C:) folder.

6. Click the Staff Party button on the taskbar to redisplay its window and then click the Directions From North icon. The size of the selected document is displayed in the status bar.

7. Choose Details from the View menu. Your view of the documents in the Staff Party folder changes to look like this (we enlarged the window so that all the details are visible):

Changing the view

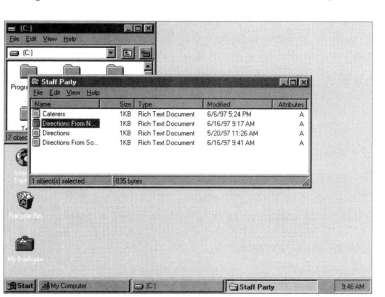

Displaying all files

When you open some folder windows, NT may not display files that are critical to its own or a program's operation, because deleting or moving these files would create havoc. If you need to, you can display these files by choosing Options from the View menu, selecting Show All Files on the View tab, and clicking OK. Remember to reselect Hide Files Of These Types in the Options dialog box when you're done.

Other views

In addition to the large-icon and details views we show here, you can view the contents of a folder window as a set of small icons or as a list, by choosing the corresponding command from the View menu. If you have turned on the folder window's toolbar (see the tip on page 68), you can use buttons to switch between views. (You may need to enlarge the window in order to display all of the toolbar buttons.)

The system folders

You can use My Computer to open the Control Panel, Printers, and Dial-Up Networking system folders. My Computer allows you to access the tools the folders contain, but you shouldn't think of these folders in the same way as the ones you create. You can't move files in or out of the system folders, for example, and you shouldn't try.

Now My Computer reports each file's size and type, as well as the date it was last modified. Notice that the contents of the (C:) window are still displayed as icons. You can change the view of one folder window independently of any others.

8. Choose List from the View menu. The window now lists the files but hides their details.

9. To open the Directions memo from this view, simply double-click the icon to the left of the document name. Then close the document again.

We'll explore some of the other features and uses of My Computer later in this chapter. For now, let's close all the folder windows. You could close them one at a time, but we'll show you a quicker way. The windows now on your screen represent nested folders: Staff Party is within (C:), which is, in turn, within My Computer. Here's how to close Staff Party, its "parent" (C:), and its "grandparent" My Computer with just one click:

Closing all related folders

1. Hold down the Shift key and click the Close button of the Staff Party window. NT closes the active window, the (C:) window, and the minimized My Computer window.

Using Windows NT Explorer

Windows NT Explorer could be called My Computer Plus. Whereas My Computer uses a series of folder windows to display the contents of your computer's storage, Windows NT Explorer uses one window divided into two panes. If you are familiar with the Windows 3.x File Manager, you'll recognize Windows NT Explorer, but at first you may be frustrated because it doesn't work in exactly the same way. Once you get used to Windows NT Explorer, however, you may abandon My Computer in favor of Explorer's power and efficiency. To see why, start the program now:

Starting Windows NT Explorer

1. Click the Start button, display the Programs submenu, and then click Windows NT Explorer to display the window shown at the top of the facing page.

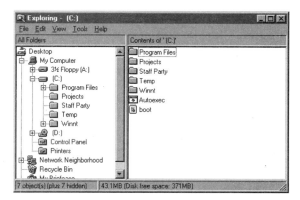

Notice that the pane on the right looks similar to the list view of a folder window displayed in My Computer.

2. Choose Toolbar from the View menu to display the toolbar, and then click the Large Icons button, which is just visible at the right end of the toolbar. Now the right pane's similarity is even more pronounced:

The Large Icons button

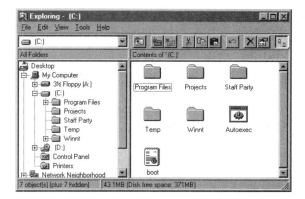

The most obvious difference between My Computer and Windows NT Explorer is the addition of the left pane, which always displays a hierarchical diagram of all your available storage space arranged like this:

- **Level One.** At the top is the desktop.

- **Level Two.** One level to the right are My Computer, Network Neighborhood, the Recycle Bin, and My Briefcase.

- **Level Three.** One more level to the right are your drives and the system folders (Control Panel and Printers).

Customizing Explorer

By default, NT does not display certain file types in the Exploring window. (Usually, these are files you don't want to touch anyway.) To change this as well as other viewing options (such as displaying filename extensions), choose Options from the View menu and click the View tab. Any changes you make are also implemented in the My Computer windows. Another way to change the view is to customize the Exploring window by resizing panes and columns. Simply point to the item's border and, when the pointer changes to a double-headed arrow, drag in the desired direction.

- **Level Four.** One level to the right on your C drive are all the folders stored on that drive.

You can expand and contract the diagram, displaying only the highest levels or zooming in for a closer look at folders and subfolders. (The fifth storage level, files, is displayed only in the right pane.) Let's experiment in the left pane:

1. Double-click the (C:) icon. The folder icons on your C drive disappear (collapse), and the minus symbol to the left of the (C:) icon becomes a plus symbol, indicating that the drive contains hidden folders. Because the C drive is still selected, its folders are displayed in the right pane even though they are no longer visible in the left pane, as shown here:

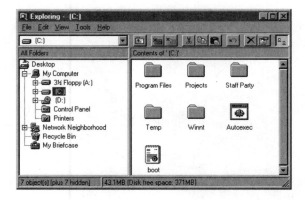

2. Double-click the (C:) icon again. The folder icons reappear (expand), and the plus symbol reverts to a minus symbol, indicating that the folders it contains are not hidden.

3. Click the Winnt folder icon once in the left pane to display the folder's contents in the right pane without expanding the diagram to display the contents in the left pane. (Notice that the folder's icon changes to an open folder.) This single-click technique is useful when you want to keep the "big picture" in view as well as see the details of a particular folder.

An open folder icon

The plus/minus symbols

Instead of double-clicking icons, you can click the plus symbol to expand and the minus symbol to contract the diagram in the left pane, without changing the view in the right pane.

You can also change the display by double-clicking icons in the right pane. Try this:

1. Double-click the Fonts folder in the right pane. Windows NT Explorer expands the diagram in the left pane to display the

Winnt folder's contents, opens the Fonts folder, and displays its contents in the right pane.

2. Click the Up One Level button on the toolbar. Windows NT Explorer closes the Fonts folder in the diagram, opens the Winnt folder, and then displays the contents of that folder in the pane on the right side of your screen. (Notice that Up One Level does not collapse the diagram in the left pane.)

The Up One Level button

3. Now click the Up One Level button again to display the contents of your C drive.

Experiment with the Exploring window until you are familiar with the various techniques for displaying the contents of folders. Then rejoin us and follow these steps to open a document and start a program from Windows NT Explorer:

1. Display the contents of the Staff Party folder.

2. Double-click the Directions icon to open the document in its associated program. Then close the document again.

3. Maximize the Exploring window and then click the Details button at the right end of the toolbar.

The Details button

4. Click the Winnt folder icon in the left pane and then scroll the right pane to check out its contents:

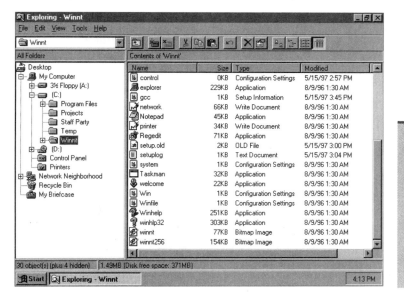

Sorting

To quickly sort files in the Exploring window, click a column header in the right pane. For example, if you click the Size header, the files are sorted with the smallest file appearing first. Click the header again to sort with the largest file appearing first.

Notice the descriptions in the Type column and the various icons to the left of the filenames.

Displaying the Welcome window →

5. Double-click the icon to the right of Welcome to start the Welcome program, which displays the window you saw when you started Windows NT Workstation 4 for the first time (see page 13). Then close the program's window.

6. End this brief tour of Windows NT Explorer by clicking the Restore button and then clicking the Close button to close its window.

You can start any program from Windows NT Explorer or from My Computer, so if a program's name does not appear on the Programs submenu of the Start menu, you can always use one of these handy helpers to track it down and start it.

Using the Find Command

The third method of locating a document you want to open or a program you want to start is to use the Find command on the Start menu. Searches performed with this command can be pretty sophisticated, but the vast majority of searches are simple attempts to locate a document based on all or part of its name. We'll show you how to conduct this type of search and leave you to explore further on your own, using the Find window's Help menu if necessary. Let's get going:

Specifying where to look

If you want to search a drive other than your C drive, click the arrow at the right end of the Look In box and select the drive from the drop-down list. If you want to search a particular folder, click the Browse button to display the Browse dialog box, where you can navigate to the folder. Click OK to return to the Find dialog box with the folder's path entered in the Look In box. (The path is then added to the Look In drop-down list so that it is available for future searches.) To search the specified drive or folder and all subfolders, be sure that the Include Subfolders check box is checked. Otherwise, NT searches only the top level of the specified drive or folder.

1. With all windows closed, click the Start button, point to Find, and then choose Files Or Folders to display this window:

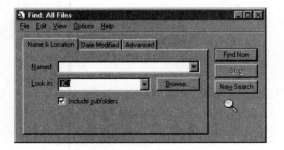

(You can also access the Find window from Windows NT Explorer by choosing Find and then Files Or Folders from the Tools menu.)

2. In the Named edit box, type *Directions*, leave all the other options as they are, and click the Find Now button to start the search. NT searches all the folders and subfolders on your C drive, and here's the result:

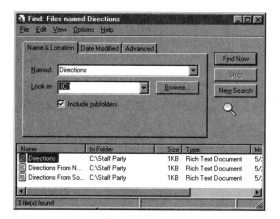

As you can see, NT finds all the documents whose names include the word *Directions*. You can select a document and use the commands on the Find window's menus to manipulate it in various ways, including printing, renaming, and opening it. (You can also open the document by double-clicking its icon.) If you are not sure which document is the one you want, you can take a peek at it, like this:

1. Right-click the icon to the left of the Directions document's name and choose Quick View from the object menu. (The command does not appear on the object menu if the selected document can't be viewed.) You see a window something like the one shown at the top of the next page.

More complex searches

In addition to searching for a document by name and location, you can search by modification date (when it was last saved) on the Date Modified tab, and by file type and size on the Advanced tab. You can even search the actual text of your documents for a particular word or phrase. For example, you could search for a Word document that you saved between May 4 and May 14, 1997 and that contains the words *Deer Creek Country Club*. You can specify that NT should find only files containing text with the exact capitalization you type, by choosing Case Sensitive from the Options menu. When you finish one search, you can start a new one by clicking the New Search button, and you can interrupt a search by clicking the Stop button. If you want to save the results of a search, choose Save Results from the Options menu. The results are saved as a file with an icon on the desktop, so the next time you need to conduct that particular search, you can double-click the icon to retrieve the results, rather than having to search all over again. (You can also choose Save Search from the File menu.)

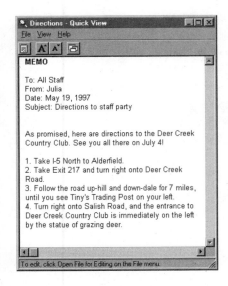

Short filenames

Long filenames work fine as long as you do all your work with Windows 95/NT programs, but if you are still using programs designed to run under MS-DOS, think carefully about the filenames you assign in NT. For example, suppose you create a Word document called 1997 Product Brochure and you later need to open it in an MS-DOS program. When you look for the document while working in that program, you'll see the filename 1997PR~1.DOC. NT converts the filename to eight characters, filling in the space, using a tilde (~) to indicate that it has truncated the name, and unhiding the three-character extension. If you have several documents with long filenames that start with the same eight characters (1997 Product List, 1997 Product Reviews, 1997 Product Proposals, and so on), they will be distinguished only by the number added to each filename (1997_PR~1.DOC, 1997_PR~2.DOC, and so on) at which point it becomes hard to know at a glance which document is which. So if you need to work with documents in both Windows 95/NT and MS-DOS programs, try to assign filenames that will work well in both environments. (You can see what the short filename will be by right-clicking the document in My Computer or Windows NT Explorer, choosing Properties, and checking the MS-DOS Name setting.)

2. This is the document you want, so choose Open File For Editing from Quick View's File menu to open the document in its associated program. Then close the document again.

3. Click the Find window's Close button to close the window.

Organizing Folders and Files

As you have seen, using icons to perform common operations makes them less intimidating than having to remember commands. And the real strength of NT becomes apparent when you use it to organize your folders and files by moving, copying, and deleting them.

Deciding on a System

Before you practice creating folders and moving documents, you might want to make a few decisions about what your folder and document structure should look like. When Windows NT Workstation 4 was installed on your computer, various folders were created on your hard drive to hold all the NT files. If you install a program under NT, that program will probably also create folders. Our concern here is not with these program folders. In fact, unless you really know what you're doing, it is probably best to leave these program folders alone. Our concern is instead with the folders you will create to hold your own documents.

Because you can use long folder names and filenames with NT, you might think it would be easy to name documents so that they are readily identifiable later. And there's no question that being able to use several words helps. Gone are the days when you had to convey the content of a document with a filename of no more than eight characters. Nevertheless, coming up with a few rules for naming files is a must. If you have ever wasted time trying to locate a document, you will probably find that spending a few minutes now deciding how to avoid such incidents in the future will more than repay you in increased efficiency. And a file-naming convention is a must if more than one person on your network works with the same set of documents.

However you decide to set up your folder structure, we strongly recommend that you store all the folders and documents you create in a folder called My Documents. (If Microsoft Office is installed on your computer, you probably already have a My Documents folder on your C drive, and you can use that.) This precaution greatly simplifies the backing up of your work because you can back up the folder and all its subfolders in one operation (see page 83 for more information). We also recommend that, to the extent possible, you use some unique document identifier at the beginning of each filename, especially if the document is likely to be used with a program that can handle only eight-character filenames (see the tip on the facing page).

Otherwise, there are no hard and fast rules for organizing documents, and the scheme you come up with will depend on your company's requirements and the nature of your work. For example, if your documents are client-based, it makes sense to identify them by client. You might use the date as the document's unique identifier, followed by the client's name, followed by the type of document. Thus, a filename like *5-20 Smith Letter* might designate a letter written to Smith Associates on May 20, and the filename *6-14 Smith Invoice* might designate an invoice sent to the same client a few weeks later.

Keep it simple

In an eagerness to impose structure, some people go overboard, developing convoluted naming systems and subfolder mazes in which it is easy to get lost. The result is usually as bad as no system at all, because it is then less hassle to create filenames on the fly and search a huge folder than it is to remember how the darn system works. Remember, to take advantage of the file-organization capabilities of NT, keep your system simple.

The important thing is to come up with a simple scheme and to apply it consistently. You can then use NT to manipulate the documents individually and in groups. For example, suppose you have accumulated so many documents in your client folders that you need to subdivide your client documents by type to make the documents more manageable. You can create a subfolder called *Invoices*, select all the documents in the client folder that have *Invoice* as part of their filenames, and drag all the invoice documents to the new folder. In the following sections, we'll demonstrate organizational tasks like this one by using My Computer and Windows NT Explorer.

Creating New Folders

You already saw in Chapter 2 how to create a new folder while saving a document (see page 43). Now we're going to create more folders to organize the documents you've created so far:

1. Close all open windows, start My Computer by double-clicking its icon on the desktop, and open the Staff Party folder, which is on your C drive.

2. With the Staff Party window active, choose New and then Folder from the File menu to display a new folder icon within the Staff Party window.

3. With the new folder selected, type *Directions* and press Enter.

4. Close the My Computer window to reduce screen clutter, and minimize the (C:) and Staff Party windows.

5. Start Windows NT Explorer, this time by right-clicking the My Computer icon and choosing Explore from the object menu. (The Explore command appears on many object menus to make the Exploring window readily available.)

6. Double-click the (C:) icon to display its folders.

7. If you do not have a My Documents folder on your C drive, make sure (C:) is selected and choose New and then Folder from the File menu. Name the new folder *My Documents*.

8. Minimize the Exploring window.

Arranging icons

If you create several new folders or move/copy several folders and documents, folder windows can get pretty untidy, making particular objects hard to find. To straighten up the active folder, you can use the techniques that you used for the desktop on page 14. Choose Arrange Icons and then By Name from the View menu. (You can also arrange by type, size, and date.) NT puts your folders first, followed by your documents. Choose Arrange Icons and then AutoArrange to have NT do this bit of housekeeping every time you make a change to the folder's contents. (AutoArrange is only available with Large Icons or Small Icons view, not with List or Details.)

Specifying What You Want to Work With

Having created the new folders, we're ready to select the documents we want to move or copy into them. You've already seen how to click an icon to select it. Here, we'll show you a few other ways of selecting that work in both My Computer and Windows NT Explorer:

1. Click the Staff Party button on the taskbar.

2. Click the first document icon, hold down the Shift key, click the last document icon, and release Shift. The entire set of documents is now selected. In the status bar, the number of selected documents and their total size is displayed:

3. Hold down the Ctrl key, click the Directions document icon, and release Ctrl. That icon is no longer part of the selection.

4. Click the Directions folder icon. Now only that icon is selected.

5. Choose Invert Selection from the Edit menu to deselect the selected icon and select the other icons in the window. (This command deselects everything that was selected and selects everything that wasn't. It's convenient when a folder contains many documents and you want to select all but a few of them.)

6. Click an empty area of the window to deselect everything.

If a My Computer folder window or the right pane of the Exploring window displays large icons, you can drag a selection rectangle around the icons of the files you want to work with. Point close to, but not at, the first icon, hold down the left mouse button and drag to the last icon. The rectangle expands as you drag, highlighting each icon it encloses. Release the button when everything you want is selected.

Shift vs. Ctrl

When selecting objects in a folder window or Windows NT Explorer, holding down Shift while clicking extends the selection to include all the objects up to and including the object you clicked last. For example, if the second object is selected, holding down Shift and clicking the fourth object extends the selection to include the second, third, and fourth objects. Holding down Ctrl while clicking adds only the clicked object to the selection. For example, if the second object is selected, holding down Ctrl and clicking the fourth object adds the fourth object, so that the second and fourth objects are selected but not the third. Holding down Ctrl while clicking a selected object removes that object from the selection without deselecting anything else.

Moving and Copying Folders and Files

As a demonstration, we are going to move the Staff Party folder into the My Documents folder and then copy documents from the Staff Party folder to the new Directions subfolder. Follow these steps:

1. Activate the (C:) window and make sure you can see both the My Documents and Staff Party folders. (Resize the window if you can't.)

Moving folders ▶ 2. Click the Staff Party folder icon to select it, and using the *right* mouse button, drag the dotted image of the selected icon over the My Documents icon. (The destination icon changes color when the pointer is in the correct place.) When you release the mouse button, you see this object menu:

Right-dragging vs. left-dragging

Dragging with the right mouse button gives you a chance to pause and think what you want to do before you do it, and you can cancel the operation if you change your mind. If you know what you're doing, you can simplify the process by dragging with the left mouse button. If necessary, you can always reverse a move or copy by choosing Undo from the Edit menu of either the source or the destination window.

3. Choose Move Here to move the folder and its contents. The Staff Party icon disappears from the (C:) window, the Staff Party window disappears from the desktop, and its button disappears from the taskbar.

4. To verify that the folder and its documents have actually moved, double-click the My Documents folder to display its contents in a window, like this:

Next, we'll use Windows NT Explorer to move a document to the new Directions folder, and then we'll copy another document. The secret to efficient moving and copying in the Exploring window is to make sure the destination folder is visible before you select the folder or document you want to move or copy. Try this:

1. Click the Exploring button on the taskbar and double-click My Documents in the left pane.

2. Double-click the Staff Party folder icon in the left pane and then select Directions From North in the right pane.

Moving documents

3. Using the *left* mouse button, drag the dotted image of the selected document over the Directions folder in the left pane. When you release the mouse button, the Directions From North icon disappears from the right pane.

4. Select Directions From South, hold down the Ctrl key, and using the *left* mouse button, drag the dotted image of the selected icon over the Directions folder. (As you drag, a plus sign is displayed below the pointer to indicate that you are copying the document, not moving it.) Release the mouse button and then release the Ctrl key. This time, the selected document's icon remains in the right pane. (If you release the Ctrl key first, NT moves the document instead.)

Copying documents

Copying vs. moving

When you use the left mouse button to drag a folder or document to a new location on the same drive, NT moves the object, unless you hold down the Ctrl key, in which case it copies the object. When you use the left mouse button to drag between drives, NT copies the object, unless you hold down the Shift key, in which case it moves the object. If you find this logic confusing, use the right mouse button to drag so that you can choose the correct action from the object menu.

5. Double-click the Directions folder icon to display its contents, and verify that the moved and copied documents are safely stored in their new folder, as shown on the next page.

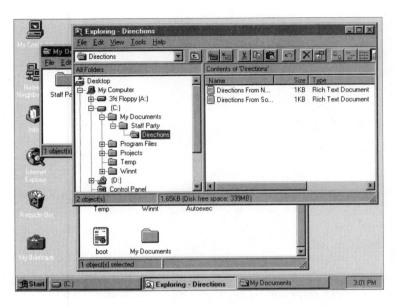

Here's how to copy a document within the same folder:

Copying documents with
the Copy command

1. Right-click the Directions From North icon in the right pane and choose Copy from the object menu. Windows puts a copy of the document on the Clipboard.

2. Right-click the Directions folder in the left pane and choose Paste from the object menu. NT pastes a copy of the Clipboard's contents back into the Directions folder, naming the new document *Copy Of Directions From North*. (To widen the Name column so that you can see the entire name, double-click the border between the Name and Size column headers.)

You can use this same technique to copy documents from one folder to another. Try it with My Computer:

Copying/moving to another computer

For security reasons, you can copy and move files to another computer on your network only if you have permission to do so. For example, you may be allowed to copy files to a file server. See page 92 for information about network security.

1. Activate the My Documents window by clicking its button on the taskbar, and open the Staff Party folder by double-clicking it. Then right-click the Directions document icon and choose Copy from the object menu.

2. Right-click the Directions folder icon and choose Paste from the object menu.

3. Double-click the Directions folder icon to see the results. As you can see here, you now have four documents in this folder:

Copying Files to and from Floppy Disks

If you work on more than one computer or share documents with colleagues but you are not on a network, you need to use floppy disks to get documents from one computer to another. You might also want to copy documents to floppy disks as a way of backing up your work (see below). The first step in copying a document to a floppy disk is to insert a formatted disk in the appropriate drive, so let's take a detour to discuss how to format floppy disks. To practice formatting, you'll need a floppy disk that is either new or that contains information you don't mind losing (formatting destroys any data already stored on the disk). Then follow these steps:

1. Minimize the Directions window and close any other open windows. Then double-click My Computer on the desktop.

2. Insert a disk in the floppy drive and right-click the drive's icon in the My Computer window to display its object menu.

← Formatting floppy disks

Backing up

Many companies require that sensitive data be stored on a file server so that it can be centrally backed up. However, personal files are usually your own responsibility. If you have a tape drive, you can use NT's Backup program. To access this program, click the Start button and choose Administrative Tools and then Backup from the Programs submenu. Insert a tape into the drive and then, if necessary, choose Erase Tape from the Operations menu. Once the tape is erased, choose Drives from the Window menu to display a list of drives. To back up an entire drive, click its check box. Otherwise, double-click the drive and navigate to the folder(s) you want to back up. Click the Backup button and change any options in the Backup Information dialog box. Then click OK to begin the procedure. If you don't have a tape drive, you will need to copy your files to a floppy disk. Either way, the backup process will be easier if you store all of your personal files in the same folder.

More about formatting

You can format a floppy disk in Windows NT Explorer using the same procedure as in My Computer. Right-click the drive's icon and choose Format. If you want to format a FAT disk as NTFS (see the tip on page 95), change the File System setting. To assign a label to the disk, type it in the Volume Label edit box. To format a disk quickly, click Quick Format to erase the disk's file record without actually erasing the files themselves.

Using Briefcase

If you frequently work on more than one computer—a desktop machine and a laptop, for example—you can use Briefcase to keep your documents in sync. To use Briefcase, right click a blank area of the desktop of the source computer and choose New and then Briefcase from the object menu. Name the briefcase to reflect what you are going to put in it and then start Windows NT Explorer. Drag the documents to the new briefcase icon on the desktop, and then drag the briefcase icon to the desired drive in the left pane of the Exploring window; for example, to the floppy drive. (NT prompts you to insert a new disk if the briefcase won't fit on one disk.) The icon disappears from the desktop. On the destination computer, open Windows NT Explorer and drag the briefcase to the desktop, where NT creates an icon for it. Double-click the icon to open the briefcase window, double-click the document you want to work on to open it, make your changes, and save the document in the briefcase. To move the documents back to the original computer, drag the briefcase icon back to the desired drive, and on the original computer, drag the briefcase to the desktop. Double-click its icon, select the files you changed on the other computer, choose either Update Selection or Update All from the Briefcase menu, and click Update to confirm that you want the file on the original computer to reflect the work you did on the other computer.

3. Choose Format from the menu to display this dialog box:

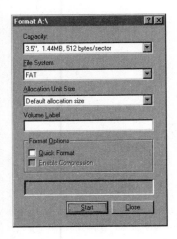

4. Check that the value in the Capacity box is correct for the disk you are formatting. (You can select a different capacity from the drop-down list.)

5. Leave the other options as they are and click Start.

6. Click OK to acknowledge that formatting will erase any data on the disk. NT quickly formats the disk, displaying its progress in the bar at the bottom of the dialog box.

7. When NT displays a message that formatting is complete, click OK to close the message box, and then close the Format dialog box.

You are now ready to copy the Directions documents to the formatted disk. Here are the steps:

1. Click the Directions button on the taskbar and if necessary, arrange the windows so that you can see the floppy drive icon in the My Computer window when the Directions window is active.

2. Choose Select All from the Directions window's Edit menu to select all four documents, point to one of the selected icons, and using the left mouse button, drag the selection over the floppy drive icon in the My Computer window. Release the mouse button. While Windows copies the documents, it

displays a progress box with documents flying from one folder to another.

3. Verify that the documents have been copied successfully by double-clicking the floppy drive icon to display its window, as shown here (your window may have a different view):

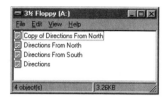

4. Remove the disk and put it to one side for now. (You will use it again later in this book.)

You can copy files in the other direction (from a floppy disk to a folder on your hard drive) using this technique, and you can also copy in both directions using Windows NT Explorer.

Renaming Folders and Files

During the course of your work, you will sometimes want to change a filename. For example, suppose you want all the filenames of the documents in the Directions folder to start with a unique word. Try these four methods of renaming the documents:

1. Close the floppy drive and My Computer windows, leaving only the Directions window open.

2. Right-click the Directions document icon, choose Rename from the object menu, type *West Directions* as the new name, and press Enter.

3. Select the Copy Of Directions From North icon, choose Rename from the window's File menu, type *East Directions*, and press Enter.

4. Select the Directions From North icon, press the F2 key, type *North Directions*, and press Enter.

Copying entire disks

To copy the contents of one disk to another disk, right-click the source drive's icon in My Computer or Windows NT Explorer and choose Copy Disk from the object menu. Select the drive you want to copy from in the first box and the drive you want to copy to in the second box. (If you are using the same drive for both disks, select it in both boxes.) Then click the Start button. NT walks you through the rest of the process. Note that both disks must be the same type and format.

5. Finally, select the Directions From South icon, wait a second, then point to its name and click again to activate the name, type *South Directions*, and press Enter. Here are the results:

You can use any of these methods to rename folders, and the methods all work equally well in Windows NT Explorer.

Deleting and Undeleting Folders and Files

If you followed along with the previous examples, you now have two extraneous documents in the Staff Party folder. The potential for confusion is obvious, so let's throw out these duplicates using Windows NT Explorer:

1. Minimize the Directions window and then start Windows NT Explorer.

The Delete button

2. Display the contents of the Staff Party folder in the right pane, select the Directions document, and click the Delete button on the toolbar. NT displays this dialog box:

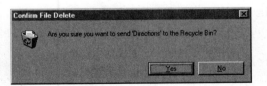

3. Click Yes to send the document to the Recycle Bin.

4. Next, right-click the Directions From South document and choose Delete from its object menu.

5. Again, confirm the deletion when prompted.

Deleting without recycling

If you know you will never need a document that is stored on your hard drive again, you can delete it permanently by holding down the Shift key while pressing the Delete key. This action is not reversible, so always think carefully before performing a deletion this way.

You can also make your selection and press the Delete key. And any of these techniques can be used to delete a folder, its subfolders, and its documents with a couple of mouse clicks. A great shortcut, you might think. But it's wise to inspect the contents of not only the folder you are considering deleting but also all its subfolders before carrying out this type of wholesale destruction.

Fortunately, NT provides a safeguard against the nightmare of inadvertently deleting vital documents. When you delete objects from your hard drive, NT doesn't really delete them. As you have seen, it moves them to a folder called the Recycle Bin on your hard drive instead. Until you empty the bin, you can retrieve objects you have deleted by mistake. Try this:

1. Choose Undo Delete from the Edit menu to restore Directions From South to the Staff Party folder.

Undoing deletions

You could repeat this step to undelete Directions, but instead let's go rummaging in the Recycle Bin:

1. Minimize the Exploring window and take a look at the Recycle Bin icon on the desktop, which has changed to show that it has something in it.

The full Recycle Bin

2. Double-click the Recycle Bin icon to display its window. (We resized the window to show all the details.)

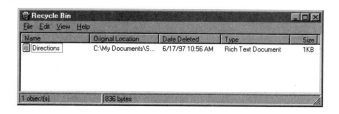

3. Right-click Directions and then choose Restore from the object menu.

4. Close the Recycle Bin window.

5. Back on the desktop, notice that the Recycle Bin icon has changed to show that the bin is empty.

How big is the Recycle Bin?

To check the size of your computer's Recycle Bin, right-click its icon and choose Properties from the object menu. By default, the bin occupies 10 percent of the hard drive on which it is stored, but you can adjust the size by moving the slider to the left (smaller) or right (bigger). If you have more than one hard drive, NT maintains a bin on each one. Click the drive tab(s) to see how big the bin is on a particular drive. To set different bin sizes for each drive, click the Configure Drives Independently option on the Global tab before adjusting the slider on each tab.

Now let's delete both documents again:

Deleting by dragging

1. Click the Exploring button on the taskbar and move the window so that you can see the Recycle Bin icon on the left side of the desktop.

2. Select the Directions From South document, hold down the Shift key, and click Directions to add it to the selection.

3. Point to the selection and drag it over the Recycle Bin icon. When you release the mouse button, NT removes the documents from the Staff Party window.

If you are deleting files to free up drive space, your efforts won't yield results until you empty your Recycle Bin. Follow these steps to remove documents from the bin and completely erase them from your hard drive:

Emptying the Recycling Bin

1. Double-click the Recycle Bin icon to open its window.

2. Select Directions, press the Delete key, and then click Yes to confirm that you want to permanently remove the document.

3. Now choose Empty Recycle Bin from the File menu to erase the remaining contents of the bin, clicking Yes to confirm your command.

Monitoring disk space

We showed you how to display a disk's free space on page 68. You can also display this and other information by right-clicking the drive icon in either My Computer or Windows NT Explorer and choosing Properties from the object menu. NT displays a dialog box with information about the disk, including its overall size and the amount of used and free space. The free/used information is also displayed visually as a pie chart.

Compressing disks

Suppose you have deleted all the files you can and you are still running out of disk space. If the disk is formatted as NTFS (see page 95 for more information), you can compress the disk to squeeze more information into the same amount of space. You can also compress specific folders. Right-click the drive or folder icon in either My Computer or Windows NT Explorer and choose Properties from the object menu. On the General tab, click the Compress check box and click OK. (Disks formatted as FAT don't have a Compress option.) NT asks whether you want to compress subfolders. If you do, click the Also Compress Subfolders option and click OK. Depending on the power of your computer, you shouldn't experience any decrease in performance from a compressed drive, even though your computer has to uncompress and compress files on the fly as you use them. To decompress the drive, you right-click, choose Properties, deselect the Compress check box on the General tab, and click OK. By the way, you cannot use MS-DOS compression utilities, such as DiskSpace, with FAT-formatted disks on NT computers.

4. Close the Recycle Bin window.

5. Scroll the left pane of the Exploring window and click the Recycle Bin icon. If the bin weren't already empty, you could also permanently delete items by right-clicking it in Windows NT Explorer and choosing Empty Recycle Bin from the object menu.

◄ Displaying the Recycling Bin in Windows NT Explorer

If you are sure you won't need to restore any of the documents in the Recycle Bin, you can empty it without checking it by right-clicking its icon and choosing Empty Recycle Bin from the object menu. Click Yes to confirm your command.

By the way, NT doesn't move objects deleted from floppy disks and the hard drives of other computers to the Recycle Bin; it actually deletes them. Always pause before clicking Yes in the Confirm File Delete message box when deleting files from anywhere but your hard drive because this type of deletion is irreversible.

◄ Deleting from floppies and drives on other computers

In this chapter, we have given you an overview of the tools NT provides to help you organize your documents so that you can quickly find them. Now it's up to you!

Working with Other Resources

4

First, we talk about NT's security system so that if you can't use a network resource, you'll know why. Then we show you how to share folders on your own computer and access files across the network. We also cover printing on both local and network printers.

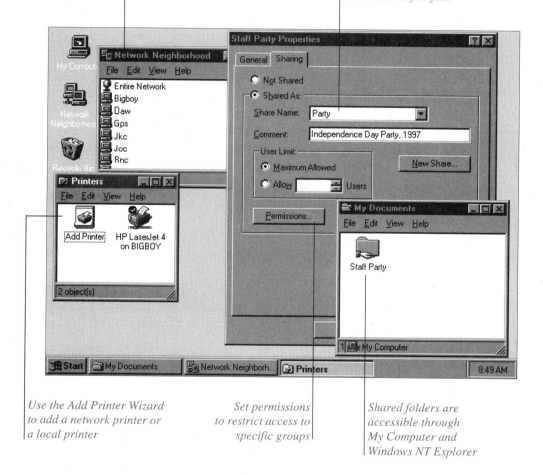

Use Network
Neighborhood to find
shared resources

Assign share names and
add comments to make
resources easy to find

Use the Add Printer Wizard
to add a network printer or
a local printer

Set permissions
to restrict access to
specific groups

Shared folders are
accessible through
My Computer and
Windows NT Explorer

So far, we have discussed working with files and folders on your own computer, but most likely you have other resources available to you (see page 7 if you need to refresh your memory about what a resource is). If you are working on a stand-alone computer, at the very least you probably have a printer, so even if you skip the discussion of using network resources in this chapter, you will want to check out the section on using printers. If you are working on a network, this chapter will show you how to work across the network to access the resources available on other computers. We also briefly cover how to monitor and control other people's use of your computer across the network. But first we take a look at network security so that if you find you can't carry out some of our instructions, you'll know why.

Understanding NT's Security

Our discussion of security in this section is primarily geared toward client-server networks, where you have no control over which computers, files, and other resources you can access, and you can't change anything. If you are working on a peer-to-peer network, you will want to check the adjacent tip for information about how to work with groups, rights, and user accounts.

Security in NT is a complicated affair, based on a system of *groups* to which *user accounts* are assigned. Different groups have different *rights*, which determine what members of each group are allowed to do within the network. In addition, different groups have different *permissions*, which determine what network resources members of each group can access. Several groups are predefined by NT, with varying levels of access. At the highest level is Administrators, an elite group reserved for network administrators with omnipotent powers. At the lowest level is Everyone, which is not so picky about its membership. In fact, by default all user accounts are initially assigned to Everyone because it has the most limited rights and permissions. Most user accounts are also assigned to a more specific group, whose rights and permissions are tailored to specific needs. And some users who don't fit neatly

Working with groups, rights, and user accounts

If you have the power, you can create a new group. Click the Start button, point to Programs, point to Administrative Tools, and click User Manager. Select the users you want to be members of the group (hold down the Ctrl key to select several users), choose New Local Group from the User menu, type a group name and description, and click OK. To add or remove users from a group, start User Manager and double-click the group name in the list at the bottom of the User Manager dialog box. To assign rights to a group, choose User Rights from User Manager's Policies menu, select a right, and then add or remove groups from the list. To create a new user account, choose New User from the User menu and fill in the requested information. Then click the Groups button and designate which group the new account belongs to and click OK twice. To edit a user account, simply double-click the account name in User Manager and make the necessary changes.

in one group or another may have their own unique combination of rights and permissions.

On a client-server network, the network administrator uses special administrative tools to set up and maintain whatever level of security the powers-that-be have deemed necessary. We can't go into much detail, but to give you an idea of what's involved, here's a brief overview:

- **Defining a domain and workgroups.** First, your network administrator organized the computers on the network into categories. Depending on the size and complexity of your company, all computers might have been assigned to a single domain or workgroup, or they might have been organized into multiple workgroups within a single domain. For example, a domain might be subdivided into workgroups called Finance, Production, Marketing, and so on.

  Domain and workgroups

- **Defining groups.** Next, your network administrator defined a set of groups that together describe all the network users in your company. This set might include various general groups predefined by NT (Power Users, Backup Operators, and so on), groups based on job function (Supervisors, Project Leaders, and so on), as well as other necessary groups.

  Groups

- **Specifying rights.** The network administrator then specified which groups had the right to perform which actions. These actions might include accessing the computers within a specific domain or workgroup, backing up the files on specific computers, resetting the system clock, and so on.

  Rights

- **Specifying permissions.** The next step was to specify which groups had permission to work with which network resources. For example, a group might have permission to use a certain printer or scanner. For resources such as a drive on a particular computer or a particular folder or file, varying levels of permission could be assigned. For example, a group might have permission to view (read) a resource but not change (write) it. Because permissions are assigned on a resource-by-resource basis, the same group might have permission to use two of a department's three printers but not the third one, for example.

  Permissions

Can you have more than one domain?

Yes, but then the network is harder to manage. The network administrator has to set up trust relationships between the domains so that they can interact. A domain with no trust relationships is called a *rogue domain* because it can lock out the administrator.

User accounts

- **Assigning users.** Finally, the network administrator set up accounts for all the network's users and assigned them to groups. Each user automatically acquired the rights and permissions assigned to his or her group. If a particular user needed additional rights or permissions, the network administrator could assign them individually to the user.

Seem like a lot of work? It is, but the result—a controlled, secure network environment—is worth it if security is critical to your company's operations. All the information about your domain's security is stored on a *domain controller*, which checks your user name and password when you log onto the network and determines what you can do with what resources. As a result, you can log on from any workstation on the network and your "security clearance" will be the same. Just remember, if you can't do something, it's probably because your job doesn't normally require that you be able to do it. It's nothing personal. And if you regularly run across tasks you think you should be able to perform but can't, you can always check with your supervisor or network administrator to ensure that you are assigned to the correct group.

Domain controller

Now let's see how you might go about using network resources, starting with drives, folders, and files.

Accessing Files Across a Network

How files are stored on a network varies with the size of the organization and other factors, such as the extent to which people need to access the same files. In some companies, each person might be assigned a "home folder" on a *file server*—a computer dedicated to the task of storing files. Everyone stores all the documents they create in their home folder so that the documents are available for use by other authorized users and can be backed up centrally. In other companies, each person might store all their documents *locally* (on their own computer) and selectively make files available to other users on the network. Still other companies might combine these two systems, distinguishing between types of files that should be stored on a file server and types that should be stored locally.

File servers

Local storage

Regardless of the storage system used, before you can access a file that is stored on another computer, the file (or the folder or drive containing it) must be *shared* with your group by its *owner*. (On an NTFS computer, files can be shared individually; on a FAT computer, all the files in a shared folder become available—you can't share individual files. See the tip below for more information about NTFS and FAT file systems.) The owner of a resource is the person responsible for it. Often the owner is the person who created the resource, but one or more groups of users might have the right to take over the ownership of a resource after it is created.

Ownership

In this section, we first look at how to share a folder that you have created on your own computer with your colleagues. (Similar techniques can be used to share drives or files.) If you don't have the right to share resources, simply read through the instructions.

Sharing Folders

Sharing a folder is easy, and because you can share folders rather than your entire hard drive, you can structure your folders so that only the information you want to share is accessible across the network. As a demonstration, suppose other people need to access the documents related to the staff

NTFS vs. FAT

Windows NT 4 can store files on your hard drive in two ways: using the File Allocation Table (FAT) method or using the NT File System (NTFS) method. The method used depends on how the hard drive is formatted. The FAT format is available under Windows NT 4 for compatibility with the MS-DOS and Windows 95 operating systems. However, for full security to be implemented under Windows NT 4, your hard drive needs to be formatted to store files using NTFS. Otherwise, someone can start your computer using a floppy disk containing the MS-DOS operating system and read the files stored on your hard drive without going through the logon procedure and passing a security clearance. Files stored on an NTFS drive can be read from the drive only by Windows NT 4. (That doesn't mean that the files can't be accessed by network computers that are running other operating systems. Those computers ask the Windows NT computer for the files, and the Windows NT computer reads them into its memory and makes them available across the network.) Other advantages of NTFS are that files are stored more efficiently, and permissions can be set for individual files. During the Windows NT Workstation 4 installation, you have the option of converting a FAT hard drive to an NTFS hard drive. If you elect not to convert at that time, the only way to make the switch later is to back up the files you want to keep, reformat the drive as NTFS, and then restore the files to the newly formatted drive. If you have a large hard drive, you might want to create a new partition and format the partition as NTFS. You can then store sensitive files in that partition and less sensitive ones in the FAT partition. Your network administrator can advise you.

party, which are stored on your computer. Here's how to make these documents available:

1. Using My Computer, display the folder window that contains the folder you want to share. In this case, display the My Documents folder window, which contains the Staff Party folder.

2. Right-click the folder that you want to share with other people (in this case, Staff Party) and choose Sharing from the object menu to display this dialog box:

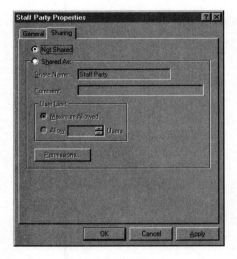

3. Click the Shared As option. The name of the selected folder appears in the Share Name edit box.

4. To give this folder a different name for sharing purposes, type *Party* in the Share Name edit box.

5. Click the Comment edit box and type any necessary identifying information. Other people will see this description when they are establishing connections to shared folders. As an example, type *Independence Day Party, 1997*.

Assigning permissions ➤ 6. Now click the Permissions button to display this dialog box:

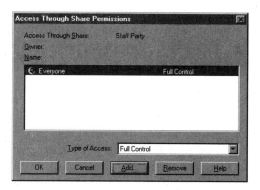

You can control which groups have permission to access the Staff Party folder by using the Add or Remove buttons.

7. Specify what type of permission the selected group has by clicking the arrow to the right of the Type Of Access box to drop down a list of settings, as follows:

- **No Access.** Shuts out the selected group of users.

←─────────── Permission types

- **Read.** Allows members of the selected group to view files in the folder but not change them.

- **Change.** Allows members of the selected group to edit the files in the folder.

- **Full Control.** Members of the selected group can edit, delete, and move files, as well as take ownership of this folder and change its permissions.

8. For this example, select Change and click OK twice to complete the sharing procedure. In the My Documents folder window, the shared folder now looks like this:

9. Hold down the Shift key and click the My Documents window's Close button to close all the My Computer windows.

Next, we'll show you how you would access this shared folder across the network.

Accessing Shared Folders

To use a file that is stored in a shared folder on another computer, we use Network Neighborhood to locate the folder and then, provided we have permission to access the folder, we can open its files by double-clicking them in the usual way. Here's how you would access the files in the Staff Party folder if they were stored on another computer:

Network Neighborhood

1. Double-click Network Neighborhood on the desktop to open a window something like this one:

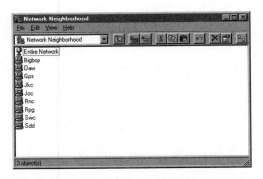

This window lists each of the computers in your domain and displays an icon for the Entire Network. (Double-clicking Entire Network shows you how your domain relates to any others on the network and is useful when you need to work across domains in large organizations.)

Accessing resources in Windows NT Explorer

You don't have to start Network Neighborhood to access a shared resource. If you prefer to work in Windows NT Explorer, you can double-click the Network Neighborhood icon in the left pane of the Exploring window to display the domain's computers, and then navigate to the shared resource in the usual way.

2. Double-click the computer on which the folder you want to connect is stored. (We double-clicked Jkc.) Party is the only shared folder on this computer, so the window looks like this:

3. Double-click the shared folder to display this window:

You can now work with the documents in the folder just as you would work with files on your own computer. Try this:

1. Double-click the Caterers icon to open the document in your word processor.

2. Close all open windows except Network Neighborhood.

If you work on a very large network, you can avoid having to traipse through all the icons in Network Neighborhood when you want to access a folder, by creating a shortcut to the folder on your desktop. However, if you want to be able to access the folder when the desktop is obscured by programs or other windows, you will want to "map" the folder to a drive letter on your computer so that the folder is readily available through Windows NT Explorer or the Open dialog boxes of many programs. Here's how to map a folder to a drive letter:

1. Choose Toolbar from Network Neighborhood's View menu and click the Map Network Drive button. You see this dialog box:

The Map Network Drive button

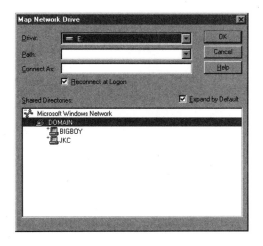

Running programs across a network

If you have permission to access a program that lives on another computer, you can run it just as you would a program that is stored on your own computer. Obviously, the program's performance across the network will depend on the power of the server where the program resides.

By default, NT enters the next available letter in the Drive box. For example, if you have two floppy-disk drives (A and B), a hard drive (C), a CD-ROM drive (D), and a Zip drive (E), NT enters F in the Drive box. You don't have to accept this suggestion. You can use any letter that isn't being used by another drive or shared folder, up to the letter Z.

2. Click the arrow at the right end of the Drive box to display a list of the available drive letters, and select a letter for the shared folder. We'll use P (for *Party*).

3. Click the Path box and then in the Shared Directories list, double-click the computer on which the Staff Party folder is stored. NT expands the Shared Directories list to display the shared resources on that computer.

4. Click Party. NT inserts the path of the folder in the Path edit box, and the dialog box now looks like this:

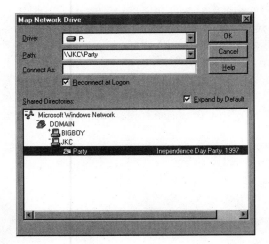

More mapping hints

The Map Network Drive button appears on the toolbars of both My Computer and Windows NT Explorer, so you don't have to start Network Neighborhood to accomplish this task. And if you decide you no longer want to map a particular drive, click the Disconnect Network Drive button in My Computer, Windows NT Explorer, or Network Neighborhood, select the drive, and click OK.

5. If you want NT to attempt to reconnect to this folder each time you turn on your computer, leave the Reconnect At Logon check box selected and then click OK. NT closes the dialog box and displays the shared folder's window and its contents.

6. Close both the folder window and Network Neighborhood.

Stopping Sharing

If you no longer want to share a folder, you can discontinue sharing by following these steps:

1. In the interests of good working relationships, warn your colleagues ahead of time that you are going to stop sharing, perhaps by sending a quick e-mail message (see page 149).

2. In My Computer or Windows NT Explorer, display the drive or folder containing the shared folder (in this case, display the contents of the My Documents folder). Right-click the shared folder, and choose Sharing from the object menu to display the dialog box shown on page 96.

3. Click Not Shared and click OK. Then close all open windows.

As you have seen, NT makes using documents on networked computers as easy as using those on your own computer, hiding all the intricacies of the network so that you can focus on your work.

Using Printers

Although computers were supposed to usher in the era of the paperless office, in our experience they have had the opposite effect. Even with the proliferation of electronic mail (see page 144) and computer-to-computer faxes, most people still need to be able to print their documents. In this section, we first look at adding and sharing a *local printer* (one that is physically connected to your computer) and then talk about using a *network printer* (one that is connected to another computer). By the way, the computer that is physically connected to the printer is called a *print server*, whether it is a local shared computer or a network computer.

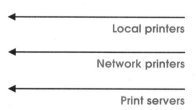

Local printers

Network printers

Print servers

Adding and Sharing a Local Printer

If you buy a new printer, you can install it for use with Windows NT Workstation 4 using the Add Printer Wizard, which is available in the Printers folder. For demonstration purposes, we are going to simulate setting up a new HP LaserJet 5/5M PostScript printer so that you do not upset your existing printer setup (if you have one). Follow these steps:

1. Click the Start button and choose Settings and then Printers from the Start menu to display a Printers folder window like the one: on the next page.

A quick way to stop sharing

The quickest way to stop sharing a folder is simply to rename it. (A network administrator can also remove all shares on a computer by renaming the computer.)

If one or more printers are already available for your computer, you will see additional icons in this window.

The Add Printer icon

2. Double-click Add Printer to display the Add Printer Wizard's first dialog box, shown here:

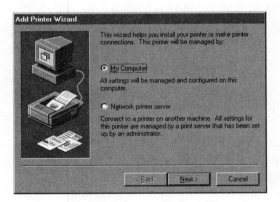

3. Click Next to tell the wizard you want to install a printer on your computer (the default option). You then see this dialog box:

Other ways to display the Printers folder

You can double-click the icon for the Printers folder in the My Computer window to open the Printers folder window. You can also display the Exploring window and then double-click the Printers folder in the left pane to display the folder's contents in the right pane.

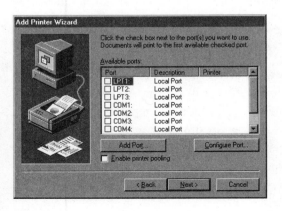

4. To set up a new printer that is physically connected to your computer via your parallel port, you would click the LPT1 (for *Line Printer 1*) check box and then click Next. For this example, scroll the Available Ports list and select FILE as the port to which the printer is connected. (Printing to a printer that is "connected" to FILE sends the printing instructions to a file on a disk instead of to the printer.) Then click Next to display yet another dialog box:

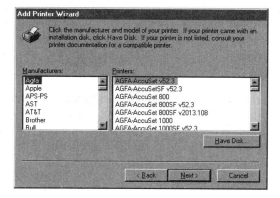

5. Scroll the Manufacturers list on the left side of the dialog box and select HP. (You can also press the H key to move down the list to the manufacturers beginning with that letter.) The Printers list on the right side of the dialog box changes to reflect the printer models manufactured by Hewlett-Packard.

6. Scroll the Printers list, select HP LaserJet 5/5M PostScript, and then click Next. The wizard displays this dialog box:

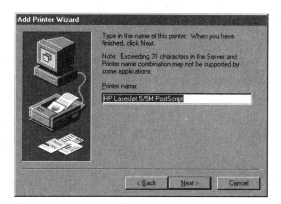

7. Type *New LaserJet* as the printer name. If another printer is
   already available, this dialog box asks whether you want
   Windows-based programs to use the new printer as the default. Click Yes to make the new printer the default printer,
   and then click Next. NT then asks whether you want to share
   this printer:

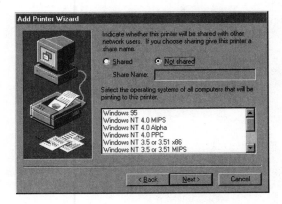

8. Click Shared and notice that the wizard truncates the printer's
   name and removes the space to comply with the MS-DOS
   eight-character naming convention. (If your network has no
   MS-DOS workstations, you can restore *New LaserJet* as the
   name.) For this demonstration, don't select any of the operating systems listed in the box below, even if you know they
   exist on your network (you will have to supply files for those
   operating systems if you do). Instead, simply click Next.

9. Click No to skip the test page and click Cancel if you do not
   actually want to install the printer. Alternatively, click Finish
   if you have your original Windows NT Workstation 4 CD-
   ROM. Windows asks you to insert the CD-ROM so that it can
   copy the necessary printer driver to your hard drive. Follow
   its instructions. You then return to the Printers folder window,
   where an icon for the new printer is now displayed, as shown
   at the top of the facing page.

Sharing an existing printer

If you want to share a printer
that is already installed on your
computer, simply right-click the
printer's icon in the Printers
folder window and choose Sharing from the object menu. You
then see a Properties dialog box
like the one shown on page 105,
with the Sharing tab selected.
Click the Shared option, assign a
share name, and click OK.

In addition to installing a new printer, you can use the icons in the Printers folder to change your printer setup like this:

1. In the Printers folder window, right-click the New LaserJet icon, choose Rename from the object menu, type *Print To FILE*, and press Enter.

Renaming printers

2. Right-click Print To FILE and choose Properties from the object menu to display this dialog box:

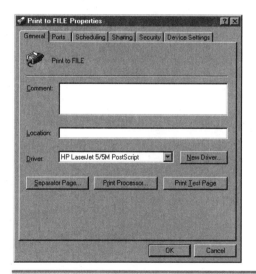

Other printer properties

Normally you will not need to bother with the other options available in the printer Properties dialog box, but a few of them might be useful. On the General tab, you can click the Separator Page button and specify a filename to have the printer print a separator page between print jobs. (You can create the page using your word processor.) You can use the Ports tab to tell NT if you switch the printer to a different port. On the Scheduling tab, you can specify whether the printer is always available or only available at certain times. (For example, you could create two icons for the same printer, designating one as *Day* and the other as *Night* and making the Night printer available only from 11 PM until 8 AM. This would enable you to send long, low-priority documents to the Night printer and have them print overnight.) You can change the permissions associated with the printer, as well as its ownership, on the Security tab, and you can also set up an audit log to see who uses the printer when.

Adding comments → 3. In the Comment box on the General tab, type *Use to create files on disk*, and click OK.

Setting the default printer → 4. If necessary, right-click the icon of the printer you usually use and choose Set As Default from the object menu to switch the default printer.

Deleting printers → 5. Right-click Print To FILE, choose Delete from the object menu, and click Yes to confirm the deletion.

Now let's see how you might connect to a shared printer.

Connecting to a Network Printer

If your computer is not directly connected to a printer, you can use the Add Printer Wizard to connect to a network printer so that you can print your documents. Connecting to a network printer is a simple matter of installing the driver for that printer on your computer. Follow these steps:

1. In the Printers folder window, double-click Add Printer to start the Add Printer Wizard, click the Network Printer Server option in the first dialog box (see page 102), and click Next to display this dialog box:

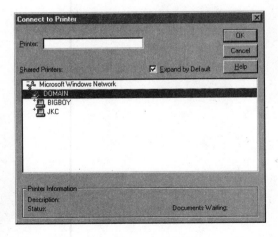

Can't see a printer?

Suppose you know that the graphics department has a superduper printer capable of producing wonderful, high-resolution, color output, and you want to use it to print a fancy invitation to a department lunch. But when you try to connect to the printer, you can't find it. You're out of luck. Only shared printers that you have permission to access will be displayed in the Connect To Printer dialog box.

2. You need to specify the location of the printer you want to connect to in the Printer edit box. To have the wizard help you with this task, double-click the computer in the Shared Printers box to which the printer is connected, and then select

the printer you want. The wizard enters the path for the specified printer, as shown here:

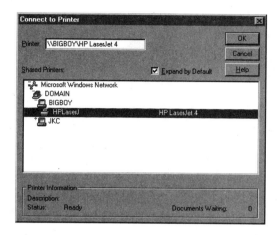

3. Click OK to close the Connect To Printer dialog box.

4. In the wizard's next dialog box, click Yes if you want this printer to be your default printer, and then click Next.

5. Click Finish to complete the installation. Its icon now appears in the Printers folder window.

6. Close the Printers folder window.

Printing Basics

Whether you attach a printer to your own computer or connect to a network printer, you follow the same basic procedure to print your documents. For convenience, NT provides several printing methods, two of which we'll briefly discuss here.

Printing from a Program

You can print an open document from within a program by using the program's Print command. (With many Windows programs, you can simply click the Print button to print the active document with the default settings.) To demonstrate, let's print the North Directions document from WordPad:

The Print button

1. Open North Directions in your word processor.

2. Choose Print from the File menu to display this dialog box, which is typical of the Print dialog box used by most Windows programs:

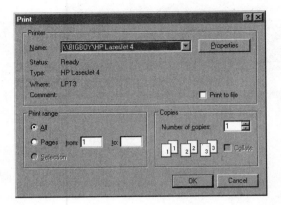

The Name box shows which printer is currently selected. The Status line tells you that this printer is ready to receive your document. The Type line tells you the type of printer, and the Where line indicates the way the printer is connected to your computer. Finally, the Comment line contains any notes about this printer (see page 105).

3. You want to print using the default printer, so leave the Name box as it is.

4. You want to print the entire document, so leave the Print Range option set to All. (With multipage documents, you can print only certain pages by clicking the Pages option and indicating the page numbers in the From and To boxes. Or you can select part of a document and print just that part by clicking the Selection option.)

5. Next, in the Copies section, change the Number Of Copies setting to 2.

6. Click OK to print two copies of North Directions on the default printer.

7. Close the document and your word processor.

Other printing options

The Print dialog box offers several printing options. For example, if you have more than one printer to choose from, you can use the Name drop-down list to select a printer other than the default one for a particular print job. The Status, Type, Where, and Comment lines then change to reflect the selected printer. You can get more details about the selected printer and change its settings by clicking the Properties button. (The Properties dialog box usually includes such settings as portrait or landscape orientation, paper size, and resolution.) Selecting the Print To File option turns the printer instructions into a file on disk instead of sending the instructions to the default location specified on the Where line. In addition to specifying the print range and the number of copies, you can tell some programs to collate multiple copies of documents that have more than one page.

Dragging a Document Icon to the Printers Folder

If you need to print existing documents and you don't want to open them first, you can drag the documents to the icon for your printer in the Printers folder. Try this:

1. Click the Start button and choose Settings and then Printers from the Start menu to open the Printers folder window.

2. Next, display the contents of the Directions folder and arrange the folder window so that you can see the printer's icon in the Printers folder window, like this:

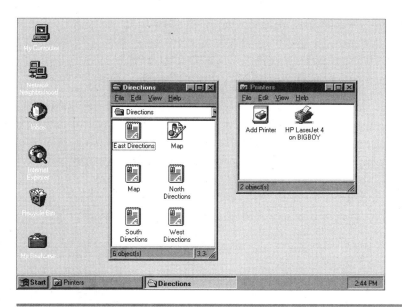

Checking the print queue

Before you print a document, you can check what the printer's current work load is. Open the Printers folder window and double-click the printer's icon to open its window, which lists current and waiting print jobs. (This list is called the *print queue* (pronounced *cue*). If the list is long or one of the print jobs is huge, you might want to use a different printer. However, if you have the necessary permissions, you can send your document to the printer and then barge ahead of other waiting documents. Print your document and then double-click the printer icon that appears at the right end of the taskbar to open the printer's window. Right-click your document in the window and on the General tab of the Properties dialog box, move the Priority slider to the right to move your document ahead of others in the queue. (For more visual control, point to the document, hold down the left mouse button, and drag the document to the desired location in the list—for example, above a huge job but below others that you know will take next-to-no-time to print.) If you send your document to the printer and, after looking at the queue, you decide to try again later, you can right-click your document and choose Cancel Printing from the Object menu. You can use the Schedule section of the Properties dialog box to print the job at a quieter time—at midnight, for example.

3. Drag the South Directions document icon to the printer's icon. NT opens the document in your word processor and prints the document (depending on the program, you may have to click OK in a dialog box). It then closes both the document and the program again.

4. Close both the Directions window and the Printers folder window.

If you often do this type of printing, you can save time by creating a shortcut to your printer on the desktop so that you don't have to open the Printers folder to print. (See page 116 for information about desktop shortcuts.)

Monitoring and Controlling Network Use of Your Computer

If you think your computer's performance is being significantly impacted by network access, you can monitor network use, disconnect a particular colleague, and even stop sharing your resources altogether. We discussed "unsharing" on page 100. Here we'll look at monitoring and disconnecting. Again, whether you can follow along with our instructions will depend on whether you have the necessary rights and permissions.

You can check who is connected to your computer's resources by following these steps:

1. Click the Start button, point to Settings, and choose Control Panel. Then double-click the Server icon to display a dialog box like this one:

2. To see which users are connected, click the Users button to display this dialog box:

Printing with the Send To command

You can print a document by right-clicking its icon in My Computer or Windows NT Explorer, choosing Send To from the object menu, and then selecting your printer. To set up Send To printing, you need to add a shortcut for your printer to your SendTo folder. See page 132 for more information.

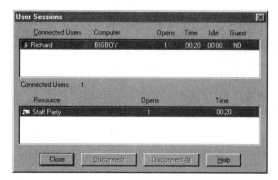

As you can see, you can disconnect selected users or disconnect all users.

3. For now, simply close the dialog box.

4. To see a list of all your shared resources and which users are connected to them, click the Shares button to display this dialog box:

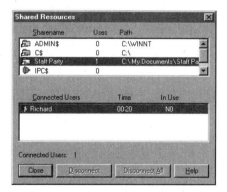

Checking all shared resources

Monitoring CPU and memory usage

If you're interested, you can take a look at how much of your computer's CPU capacity and memory are being used at any given time. In the tip on page 57, we told you how to use the Windows NT Task Manager to shut down programs that are misbehaving. Task Manager also tracks the processes that your CPU performs and how much CPU capacity and memory they use. To display Task Manager, right-click a blank area of the taskbar and choose Task Manager from the object menu, or press Ctrl+Alt+Delete and click the Task Manager button in the Windows NT Security dialog box. Click the Processes tab to see what programs are currently running on your computer. Most of them have been started by NT, not you, and even through they may currently be idle (a CPU value of 0), they still occupy space in your computer's memory. Click the Performance tab to see the total CPU and memory usage. To keep Task Manager close at hand, click the Minimize button at the right end of its title bar. The window shrinks to a program button on the taskbar, but also displays a small box to the left of the clock. You can point to the box at any time to display the CPU usage.

You can disconnect one or all users from a selected resource.

5. Again, click Close.

Checking shared resources
in use

6. To see a list of only the shared resources to which users are currently connected, click the In Use button to display this dialog box:

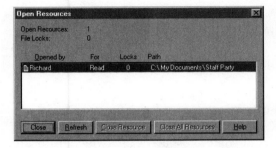

As you can see, this dialog box displays not only connections to shared folders but also connections to the individual files within the folders. You can force a selected user to close a resource or force all users to close all resources.

7. Click Close, click Cancel to close the Server dialog box, and then close Control Panel.

This concludes the first part of our book. You now know enough about Windows NT Workstation 4 to accomplish daily tasks, but there's a lot more to learn. Part Two helps you build proficiency by taking advantage of the many other features of NT.

PART TWO

BUILDING PROFICIENCY

In Part Two, we build on the techniques you learned in Part One to round out your NT skills. After completing these chapters, you will be able to put NT to work, streamlining your daily tasks and facilitating communication both within your company and with the outside world. In Chapter 5, you use some simple NT techniques to increase your efficiency when working with programs and documents. In Chapter 6, you explore the world of communications, including company e-mail, the Internet, and Internet e-mail. In Chapter 7, you look at the many ways you can customize your on-screen display and your computer setup to suit your needs.

5 Increasing Your Efficiency

We create shortcut icons for programs and folders on the desktop and then add shortcuts to the Start menu, the Programs submenu, and the Startup submenu. Finally, we show you some handy techniques for speeding up everyday tasks.

Create shortcut icons to files, folders, and programs for easy access from the desktop

Create a new, blank document directly on the desktop

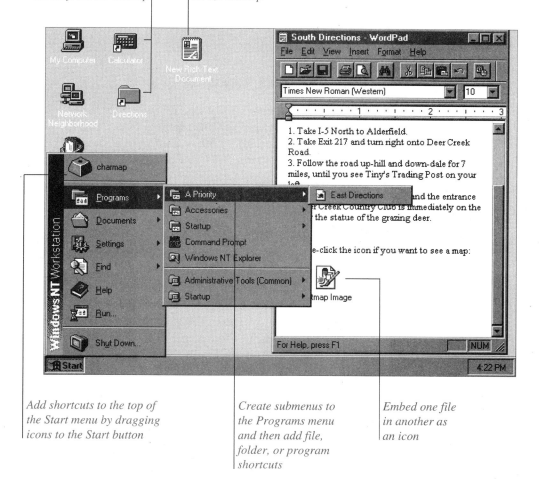

Add shortcuts to the top of the Start menu by dragging icons to the Start button

Create submenus to the Programs menu and then add file, folder, or program shortcuts

Embed one file in another as an icon

Part One showed you how to accomplish basic NT tasks and gave you enough information to start working in this new environment. By now you've probably experimented a bit, and you're ready to move on to more complex tasks. In this chapter, we focus on how to take advantage of Windows NT Workstation 4 to get your work done efficiently.

Getting Going Quickly

You've learned how to start a program by choosing it from the Programs submenu of the Start menu. You've also learned how to start a program and open a document at the same time using the following methods:

- **The Documents submenu.** Click the Start button, point to Documents, and choose the one you want.

- **The My Computer, Windows NT Explorer, or Find window.** Locate and double-click the document. (You can also start a program by double-clicking its icon in these windows.)

All of these methods of getting down to work require several steps, but with NT, you can speed things up by making the programs and documents you use most frequently immediately accessible. In this section, we'll examine a few simple techniques to provide instant access.

Using Shortcut Icons

For the ultimate in convenience, you can create a shortcut to any program, folder, or document and place an icon representing the shortcut on the desktop. Then double-clicking the icon starts the program, or takes you directly to the folder's window, or opens the document, depending on the nature of the shortcut.

Creating Shortcut Icons

To demonstrate, we'll create a shortcut icon on the desktop for the Calculator program you used in Chapter 2. Follow these steps:

Ready-made shortcuts

If you install a new program on your computer, the program's setup utility may create desktop shortcuts and Start menu shortcuts for you. If your desktop and Start menu become cluttered with shortcuts you rarely use, you can discard them without affecting their programs in any way (see pages 120 and 126).

1. Double-click My Computer on the desktop and then choose Options from the View menu to display this dialog box:

Changing the My Computer display options

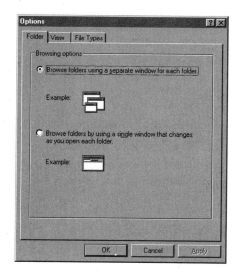

2. To have My Computer display the contents of folders in one window instead of opening a separate window for each folder, select the bottom (single-window) option and click OK.

Using a single window

3. In the My Computer window, double-click the (C:) icon to display its contents in the window, then double-click the Winnt icon to display its subfolders and files, and finally, double-click the System32 icon.

4. Scroll the System32 folder window to find the Calc (for *Calculator*) program.

Creating icons for programs

5. Point to the Calc icon, and using the right mouse button, drag the dotted image of the icon up and onto the desktop, releasing the mouse button when the image is to the right of the My Computer window.

The Calc icon

6. Choose Create Shortcut(s) Here from the object menu. NT adds the shortcut icon to the desktop, as shown on the next page.

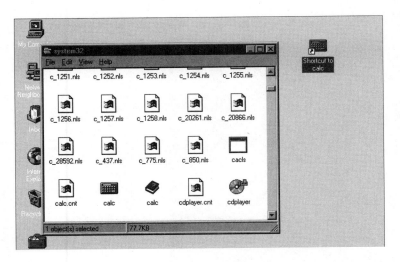

Renaming icons

7. The arrow in the bottom left corner of the icon tells you that double-clicking this icon is a shortcut for starting the program called *Calc*, so you don't need the word *Shortcut* in the name. To change the name, click the icon to select it, then click the icon name, type *Calculator*, and press Enter.

Now let's try out the shortcut icon:

1. Double-click the Calculator shortcut icon to start the program and display the Calculator window shown earlier on page 49.

The Create Shortcut Wizard

In our example, we select an object and then specify the location for its shortcut icon. But you can also select a location and then specify the object. Simply right-click the desktop or the folder where you want to create the shortcut icon and choose New and then Shortcut from the object menu. NT starts the Create Shortcut Wizard, and you can then follow the instructions in the wizard's dialog boxes.

Program icons vs. shortcut icons

Shortcut icons are distinguished from program icons by the upward pointing arrow in the bottom left corner. Whereas program icons identify the storage locations of the programs they represent (like the numbers on a house or a sign on a building), shortcut icons are instructions to NT. For example, the program icon for the Calculator is located in the System32 folder on your C: drive if that's where the program is stored, and if you move the program to another folder, its icon moves to the new location, too. However, if you create a shortcut icon to the Calculator on the desktop, the icon doesn't indicate that the program is stored on the desktop. Instead, it stores the address of the program, and double-clicking the icon tells NT to go to that address and start the program it finds there. Each program has only one program icon, but you can create as many shortcuts to that program as you want. And when you no longer need a particular shortcut, you can simply delete it without affecting the program or its other shortcuts in any way.

2. Click the buttons for 24.99, click *, click the 4 button, and then click =. (You can also press numeric keypad keys.) The display bar shows the cost (without sales tax) of four copies of *Quick Course in Microsoft Office 97*: 99.96, or $99.96.

3. Close the Calculator by clicking its Close button.

Creating a shortcut icon to a folder or document is just as easy. As an example, let's put the Directions folder and the North Directions document within easy reach:

1. Click the title bar of the System32 folder window to make it active, and then press Backspace until the (C:) window is displayed. Then double-click first the My Documents icon and then the Staff Party icon.

Backtracking through My Computer windows

2. Using the right mouse button, drag the Directions folder icon to the desktop, choose Create Shortcut(s) Here from the object menu, and change the name of the shortcut to *Directions*.

Creating icons for folders and documents

3. Double-click the Directions shortcut icon. NT displays the Directions folder window without going through any preceding folder levels.

4. Using the right mouse button, drag the North Directions document icon to the desktop, choose Create Shortcut(s) Here from the object menu, and change the shortcut icon's name to *North Directions*. Here are the results:

Left-dragging vs. right-dragging

You may have several options when you drag an icon, but you will not find out what they are or be allowed to choose among them if you left-drag the icon. To be on the safe side, always right-drag an icon so that you can choose from the options on the object menu. If there is only one possible action, right-dragging performs it without offering an object menu.

5. Double-click the North Directions shortcut icon. NT starts your word processor and opens the document. Click the Close button to close the window again.

Creating shortcut icons within folder windows

You can create shortcut icons within folder windows as well as on the desktop. For example, to create a shortcut icon for the North Directions document in the (C:) window, you would display both the (C:) and the Directions folder windows, right-drag the North Directions icon from the Directions window into the (C:) window, and choose Create Shortcut(s) Here from the object menu.

Deleting Shortcut Icons

When you no longer need immediate access to a program, folder, or document, you can delete its shortcut icon to free up space on the desktop. Here's how:

1. Select the North Directions shortcut icon on the desktop and press the Delete key.

2. When NT asks you to confirm that you want to send the North Directions shortcut icon to the Recycle Bin, click Yes.

3. Close any open windows.

Using Start Menu Shortcuts

Shortcuts across the network

If you often open a file located on another computer, you may want to create a shortcut icon for it on your desktop to save time. Double-click the Network Neighborhood icon and locate the file. Point to it, hold down the right mouse button, and drag the file to your desktop. Release the mouse button and choose Create Shortcut(s) Here from the object menu. NT creates the shortcut. To open the file, double-click the shortcut icon. If you save changes to the file, NT knows to save the file on the originating computer.

When you are working in a maximized window, you cannot see the desktop to double-click any shortcut icons you might have placed there. In that case, you will find it quicker to access a program or document from the Start menu.

The Start menu is actually a group of shortcuts arranged in a series of submenus. You can add shortcuts to the Start menu itself or to its Programs submenu. Follow these steps:

1. Double-click the My Computer icon on the desktop to open its window, double-click the (C:) icon, double-click the Winnt icon, and then double-click the System32 icon.

2. Scroll the System32 window to find the Charmap (for *Character Map*) program.

3. Point to the Charmap icon, and using the left mouse button, drag the dotted image of the icon down onto the Start button in the bottom left corner of the screen. (Notice as you drag that an upward pointing arrow indicating a shortcut is added to the dotted image when you reach the Start button.)

Adding programs to the top of the Start menu

4. Now click the Start button. As you can see here, Character Map is now accessible from the Start menu:

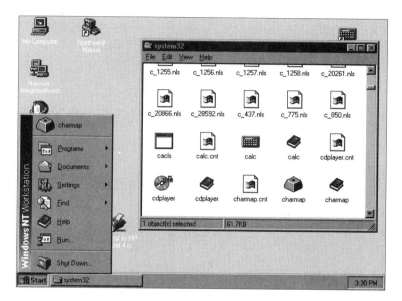

5. Close the System32 window.

Adding Shortcuts to the Programs Submenu

Suppose you want to create a submenu from which you can easily access all the important documents you are currently working on, including the Directions documents. Here's how you can include this submenu in the Start menu's Programs list and how to add a shortcut for the East Directions document to the submenu:

1. Right-click a blank area of the taskbar, choose Properties from the object menu, and click the Start Menu Programs tab in the Taskbar Properties dialog box to display the options shown on the next page.

Adding submenus to the Start menu

The Create Shortcut Wizard

2. Click the Add button. NT starts the Create Shortcut Wizard, which displays this dialog box:

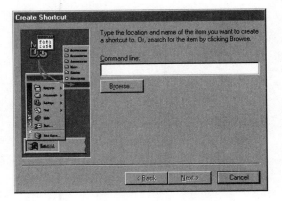

3. If you are an experienced DOS user, you can probably figure out what to type in the Command Line edit box (*C:\My Documents\Staff Party\Directions\East Directions.rtf*, but you must enclose the path of the document in quotation marks because the folder and filenames include spaces, and you must include its extension; see the tip on page 59 for information about paths). Otherwise, click the Browse button to display this dialog box so that you can look for the document:

Using the Browse dialog box

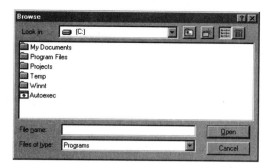

4. With (C:) displayed in the Look In box, double-click first the My Documents folder, then the Staff Party folder, and then the Directions folder.

5. Change the setting in the Files Of Type drop-down list to All Files to display the Directions folder's contents.

6. Finally, double-click the East Directions document to close the Browse dialog box and enter the path of the selected document in the Command Line edit box.

7. Click Next to display this wizard dialog box:

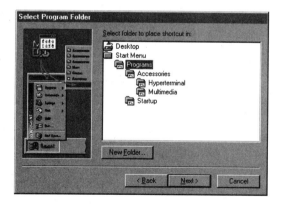

This dialog box displays all the possible locations you can select as a home for a shortcut to the specified document. Notice that Programs is the only first-level submenu of the Start menu to which you can add shortcuts.

8. With Programs selected, click New Folder to create a sub-menu for your documents. The wizard adds a new subfolder

Wizards

The NT wizards are tools that walk you through specific procedures, soliciting information so that they can take care of a lot of the grunt work for you. You don't have to use the wizards, but when you are learning NT, they are a great way to quickly carry out tasks that might otherwise be a bit confusing. If you make a wrong selection or enter wrong information while using one of the wizards, just click the Back button to retrace your steps, correct your mistake, and then click Next to move forward again.

called *Program Group (1)* within the Programs folder and places it in alphabetical order in the subfolder diagram.

Putting the submenu at the top of the list

9. Type *A Priority* as the new folder's name (we chose this name so that the new folder will be placed alphabetically at the top of the list) and then click Next to display the wizard's last dialog box:

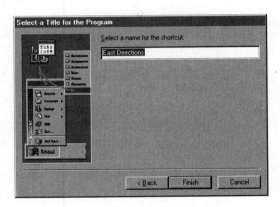

10. Click Finish and then click OK to close the Taskbar Properties dialog box.

Now for the acid test:

1. Click the Start button to display the Start menu, point to Programs, and then point to A Priority. Here's the shortcut to the document, just waiting to be clicked:

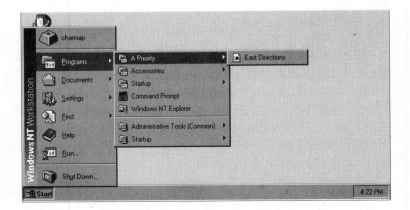

Adding Shortcuts to the Startup Submenu

When exploring the Start menu, you may have noticed the Startup submenu and wondered about its purpose. If you use a particular program in almost every computing session, you can have NT automatically start that program whenever you turn on your computer. All you have to do is put a shortcut to the program in the taskbar's Startup folder. Then when you turn on your machine, NT checks the Startup folder and starts any programs it contains without you lifting a finger.

To demonstrate, let's put a shortcut to the Calculator program in your Startup folder. Follow these steps:

1. Click the Start button, point to Settings, choose Taskbar to display the Taskbar Properties dialog box, and click the Start Menu Programs tab. (You can also right-click a blank area of the taskbar and choose Properties to display this dialog box.)

   Adding program shortcuts to the Startup submenu

2. Click Add to start the Create Shortcut Wizard and in the first dialog box, type *C:\Winnt\System32\Calc.exe* in the Command Line edit box and click Next. (You don't need to enclose the path in quotation marks because the folder and filenames have no spaces.)

3. In the second dialog box, click the Startup folder at the bottom of the list box and click Next.

4. In the last dialog box, change the name in the edit box to *Calculator* and click Finish.

5. Finally, click OK to close the Taskbar Properties dialog box.

   To test this Startup shortcut, you need to restart your computer. Follow these steps:

1. Click the Start button and choose Shut Down to display the Shut Down Windows dialog box.

2. Click the Restart The Computer option and then click Yes. NT shuts itself down, and after you log back on, you see the Calculator open on the desktop.

Another way of restarting

To shut down or restart your computer, you can press Ctrl+Alt+Delete to display the Windows NT Security dialog box. Click the Shut Down button, select either the Shutdown or Shutdown And Restart option, and click OK. The Windows NT Security dialog box also gives you access to Task Manager (see page 111), allows you to lock your workstation or log off so another user can log on (see page 29), and enables you to change your password (see page 9).

Removing Start Menu Shortcuts

You now have instant access to the Calculator through two shortcuts: the desktop icon and the shortcut on the Startup submenu. Let's remove the shortcut from the Startup submenu (you can use this technique to remove any Start menu shortcut):

1. Right-click a blank area of the taskbar, choose Properties, and click the Start Menu Programs tab.

2. Click the Remove button to display this dialog box:

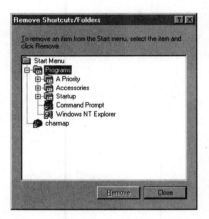

Rearranging Start-menu shortcuts

If you add a shortcut to the Start menu and later decide you want to move it, right-click a blank area of the taskbar to display the Taskbar Properties dialog box, click the Start Menu Programs tab, and then click the Advanced button. Windows NT Explorer starts and configures the Exploring window to display the contents of the Start Menu folder, which is buried deep inside the Winnt folder. You can then use normal Explorer techniques (see page 70) to display the contents of subfolders and move, copy, rename, and delete shortcuts.

3. Double-click the Startup folder and select Calculator.

4. Click the Remove button and click Yes to confirm that you don't want the shortcut any more.

5. Click Close to close the Remove Shortcuts/Folders dialog box, and then click OK to close the Taskbar Properties dialog box. Notice that removing the shortcut from the Startup menu has not closed the Calculator window, nor has it in any way affected the Calc program stored on your hard drive.

6. Close Calculator.

Working Smart

Hungry for more ways of speeding up your daily work? This section looks at several techniques for working with documents that take advantage of some nifty built-in NT capabilities. We'll use the WordPad and Paint programs for our examples, but bear in mind that you can use the same techniques with many commercial programs designed to work with Windows NT Workstation 4.

Creating Instant Documents

You can start a new, blank document with a couple of clicks of the mouse button, without even opening the document's program. Here's how:

1. Right-click a blank area of the desktop and point to New to display a submenu something like the ones shown here:

   Creating a new document on the desktop

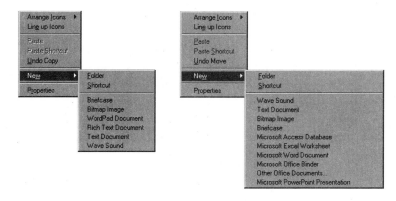

The menu on the left is for a "bare bones" NT installation, and the one on the right is from a system on which Microsoft Office 97 has been installed. As you can see, the Office programs have been added to the New submenu, so that you can create new office documents this way.

2. If you have a Rich Text Document item on your submenu, choose it. Otherwise, choose your word processor. NT displays on the desktop an icon something like the one shown on the next page.

3. Rename the icon as *Map*, retaining the *rtf* extension if it is already there (see page 130 for a discussion of extensions).

4. Double-click the icon. NT starts your word processor and opens the blank Map document.

5. Type *Here is a map to the Deer Creek Country Club:* and save the document, using Save As instead of Save and making sure that the Save As Type setting is Rich Text Format.

6. Close the WordPad (or your word processor) window.

For good measure, let's create another instant document, this time in a folder:

Creating a new document in a folder

1. Double-click the Directions shortcut icon on the desktop to display the Directions folder window.

Two documents with the same name?

You may wonder how we can create two files with the exact same name (Map). Actually, the names aren't exactly the same, because the files have different extensions that tell NT what type of program created the file. For more informantion about extensions, see the tip on page 130.

2. Right-click a blank area of the folder window and choose New and then Bitmap Image from the object menu. Then rename the icon as *Map*.

3. Double-click the icon to both start your graphics program and open the blank Map graphic document. (If you have no other graphics program on your computer, Paint, the program that comes with NT, opens.)

4. Use the Pencil and Text tools to create a map like this one:

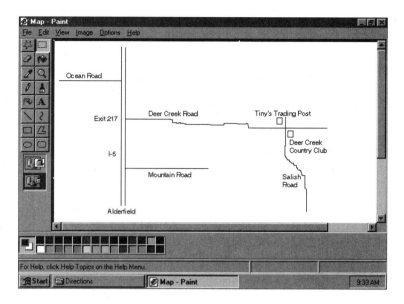

You can hold down the Shift key while dragging the Pencil tool to draw straight lines. If you don't know how to work with the Text tool, don't worry about including the street names. The goal here is not to teach you how to use Paint (you can read the tip below and experiment on your own) but to create a simple graphic for future examples.

5. Save the graphic and close the Paint window.

Next, we'll use the two documents you just created to demonstrate a few other ways to save time by working smarter.

Using Paint's tools

The Paint program offers lots of tools to help you create your own works of art. Before selecting any tool, you should first select a color from the color palette at the bottom of the Paint window. Next, click the drawing tool you want in the tool box along the left side of the window. Included are tools for drawing pencil-drawn lines, brushed lines, airbrushed lines, straight and curved lines, and various geometric shapes, as well as a text tool. To zoom in for a closer look at a section of your drawing, click the Magnifier tool and then click the area you want to examine. You can change the zoom percentage by selecting a magnification from the list below the tool box. (This list has different options depending on the tool selected.) To zoom back out, click the Magnifier tool again and then click your drawing. To change an object's color, click the Fill With Color tool, select a color from the color palette, and then click the object. To cut or copy part of a drawing, use either the Free-Form Select or Select tools to drag a border around the object, and then choose Cut or Copy from the Edit menu. To erase part of a drawing, use the Eraser tool. If you want to stretch or rotate the drawing, experiment with the commands on the Image menu. If you make a mistake, you can undo the last action by choosing Undo from the Edit menu. To save, open, or print a Paint file, follow the same proceedure you would for any other NT program.

Associating Documents with Programs

The tip way back on page 65 explained that you can often double-click a document's icon to both open the document and start its program because NT keeps a list of which file types belong to, or are *associated* with, which programs. Sometimes NT cannot open a document because it has no record of a particular file type. Instead, it displays an Open With dialog box and asks you to select the program you want to use to open the document. And sometimes NT's list tells it to open the document with a different program from the one you want. In either case, you'll need to set the record straight. Follow the steps below to ensure that Rich Text Format documents, which are identified by the rtf extension after their filenames, are opened with WordPad, and that Bitmap Image documents, which are identified by the bmp extension, are opened with Paint. (See the adjacent tip for more information about extensions.)

Extensions

An extension is a three-character suffix added to the end of a filename and separated from the name by a period. Extensions are not case-sensitive; rtf and RTF are considered to be the same. Back in the old days of MS-DOS eight-character filenames, extensions were often used to categorize and identify files; for example, *ltr* might be used to identify correspondence. Because we can use long filenames in Windows NT Workstation 4, extensions now have a different purpose. NT automatically adds an extension when you save a file created in a program it recognizes, and uses this extension to identify which program to open when you double-click the file's icon. (If you manually add an extension, you will end up with two—not a good idea!) Depending on the settings in the Windows NT Explorer Options dialog box, you may or may not be able to see the extension. (See the tip on page 71 if you want to hide or display extensions.)

1. The Directions folder window should still be open on the desktop. (If necessary, click it to make it active.) Choose Options from the window's View menu and click the File Types tab to display the options shown here:

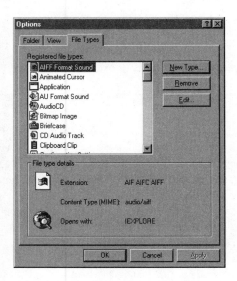

For information about the other options in this dialog box, see the tip on the facing page.

2. Scroll the Registered File Types list and select Rich Text Document. The File Type Details section tells you that this file type has an extension of RTF, that its content type is not identified (this information is used by e-mail and Internet programs), and which program will be used to open it.

3. With Rich Text Document selected, click the Edit button to display this dialog box:

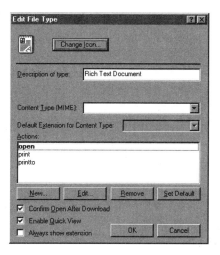

4. Click Open in the Actions list and click Edit again to display yet another dialog box:

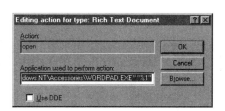

◄────────────────
Selecting an action

5. If the path in the Application Used edit box is not as follows:

   "C:\Program Files\Windows NT\Accessories\wordpad.exe" "%1"

   change it by either typing the path or using the Browse dialog box to locate WordPad. Then click OK and Close.

Other file type options

In addition to editing existing file types by clicking the Edit button, you can also add and remove file types. To add a new file type, click the New Type button. NT displays the Add New File Type dialog box, where you can enter the specifications of the new file type. To remove a file type from the Registered File Types list, select the type and click the Remove button. NT then displays a warning asking if you are sure you want to delete the type. If you know you will never need to open files of this type, click Yes.

6. If necessary, repeat steps 2 through 5 to associate the Bitmap Image file type with the Paint program. The path in the Application Used edit box should be as follows:

   "C:\WINNT\system32\mspaint.exe" "%1"

7. Click Close to close the Options dialog box, and then test your associations by opening and closing both the Map.rtf document and the Map.bmp graphic. Close the Directions folder window.

   If necessary, return these associations to their former programs when you have worked your way through the book.

Sending Documents Places

Suppose you want to move the Map document now on your desktop to the Directions folder. Because you created a shortcut to the Directions folder window, you can simply double-click the shortcut icon and then drag the Map document from the desktop into the folder window. But for demonstration purposes, we'll show you another way to accomplish the same task, by using the Send To command. To understand how Send To works, we'll first take a look at the command. Follow these steps:

1. Right-click the Map document icon on the desktop and point to Send To to display this submenu:

Other actions

The other actions listed in the Actions list of the Edit File Type dialog box are the default commands that have been defined for the selected file type. You can edit an existing command as we explain here, and really techie types can also create new commands by clicking the New button. To delete a command, select it in the Actions list and click the Remove button. To reset the list to the default commands, click the Set Default button.

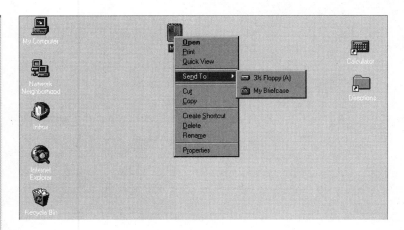

By default, the Send To command includes only these two destinations. Depending on your computer's setup, you might also have other items, such as one or more printers or an e-mail program, on your Send To submenu.

2. Click the desktop to close the object menu.

You can add items you use frequently, such as folders or programs, to the Send To submenu, by placing shortcuts to the desired destinations in your SendTo folder. This folder is part of your profile (see the adjacent tip). As a demonstration, follow these steps to locate the SendTo folder and add a shortcut to the Directions folder to it:

1. Click the Start button and choose Find and then Files Or Folders from the Start menu.

Finding the SendTo folder

2. In the Named edit box on the Name & Location tab, type *SendTo*, and with (C:) in the Look In box and Include Subfolders selected, click the Find Now button. NT then finds several SendTo folders, one for each profile on your computer. However, they all look confusingly alike.

3. Double-click the right border of the In Folder column header to expand the column. The Find dialog box now looks something like this:

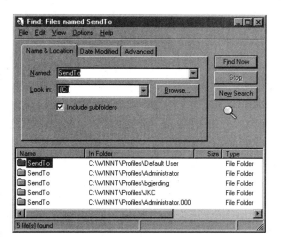

User profiles

When you customize elements such as your desktop, Start menu, or Send To command, information about the customization is stored in a file called user profile. If several user accounts can be accessed from your computer, each account has its own profile, which describes the way everything should look when the account owner logs on. By default, your user profile is *local*; and you will see your custom setup only if you log onto your usual computer. If you frequently log on from other computers, your profile can be changed to *roaming* so that you see the same setup no matter where you log on. This kind of change is usually handled by the network administrator, who will simply add the path of your user-profile file to your user account information so that the computers on the network know where to look for your profile.

4. Locate the SendTo folder designated by C:\WINNT\Profiles and your username, and double-click it to display a SendTo folder window like this one:

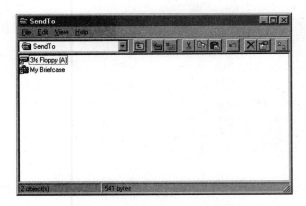

As you can see, the folder window contains a shortcut to each of the two items that were listed on the Send To submenu displayed earlier.

Adding a shortcut to the SendTo folder

5. Point to the Directions shortcut icon on the desktop, hold down the left mouse button, hold down the Ctrl key, and drag a copy of the icon into the SendTo folder window, releasing first the mouse button and then the key.

6. Close both the SendTo and the Find windows.

7. Now right-click the Map document icon and choose Send To and then Directions. Instantly, the Map icon disappears from the desktop.

8. Double-click the Directions shortcut icon to open its folder window. Verify that Map is now stored in this folder.

You can use the Send To command as an alternative to associating file types. For example, if you usually want rtf documents to be opened in your word processor but you want to open a particular rtf document in WordPad, you can add a WordPad shortcut to your SendTo folder and use the Send To/WordPad command to open the document instead of double-clicking it.

Reusing Information

If you followed along with the examples in Chapter 2, you know that reusing the same information in different documents is easy. Just select the information in the desired source document, choose Copy from the Edit menu, open the document in which you want to paste the information, click an insertion point, and choose Paste from the Edit menu.

However, the power of NT far exceeds this simple kind of copying and pasting. With NT, you can build documents that are patchworks of pieces created in different programs and that continue to be associated with the programs that created them. These "patchwork" documents are made possible by a feature called *OLE* (pronounced *olay*). The technology behind OLE is pretty complicated, but you don't have to be an OLE expert to take advantage of it. Here is a quick overview of the concept so that you can decide when and how to use it.

The *O* in OLE stands for *object*. As you know, an object is an item or an element of a document. It can be a block of text, a graphic, a table, a chart, and so on. The program that creates the object is called the *server*, and the original document is called the *source document*. The object can be used by another program called the *client*, and the client document in which the object is used is sometimes called the *container document*.

To create a patchwork document, you can *link* an object to the document (the *L* in OLE) or you can *embed* the object (the *E*). When you link an object, you need both the source document and the container document to be able to display the object. When you embed an object, it becomes part of the container document and you no longer need the source document.

← Linking vs. embedding

So how does all this influence how you go about creating patchwork documents? If the object is used in more than one document and is likely to change, it is best to create the object in its own source document and then link the object where it's needed. If the object is used in only one document or is not going to change, embedding might be the best way to go because embedded information can be edited in the container document without the source document having to be present.

OLE-supporting programs

Most recent versions of commercial Windows programs support OLE in some fashion, but not all are capable of acting both as an OLE server and an OLE client, and not all support the most recent incarnation of the OLE technology. If you are working with an older version of a favorite program, you will need to experiment to find out what its capabilities are.

Bear in mind, however, that documents that contain embedded objects can get very large.

So that's the scoop on OLE. Now let's see how you might go about using it. First, we'll embed the graphic you created in Paint in a Directions document:

Embedding an object

1. In the Directions folder window, double-click the North Directions document to open it in WordPad.

2. Maximize the WordPad window if necessary, press Ctrl+End to move to the end of the document, press Enter a couple of times, type *Here is a map:*, and press Enter twice.

3. Choose Object from the Insert menu to display the dialog box shown here:

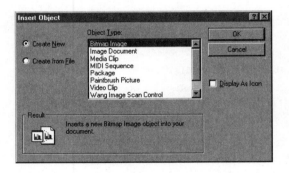

4. With Bitmap Image selected in the Object Type list, select the Create From File option and when the dialog box changes to let you enter the name of the document, click the Browse button to display the Browse dialog box.

Other programs

Although the instructions given here are specific to WordPad, the procedure is very similar for other Windows programs that support OLE. To link or embed an object in another program, look for an Object or Insert Object command and follow the directions given in the dialog box, using Help if necessary. (Some programs also forge links by means of a Paste Special command on the Edit menu.)

5. Double-click the Map graphic to return to the Insert Object dialog box with the document's path in the File edit box, and click OK. The dialog box closes, and you return to the North Directions document, where the map has been embedded in a large frame.

6. Scroll upward to see the map in place, as shown in the graphic at the top of the facing page.

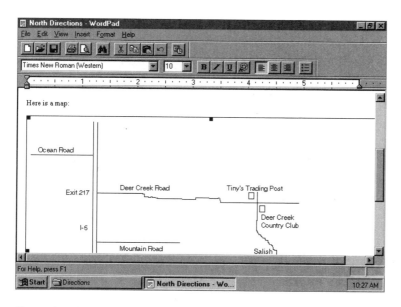

7. Save the document.

Now suppose you need to change Ocean Road in the map to Ocean Avenue. Instead of making the change in Paint and re-embedding the object in North Directions, you can change it using Paint's tools without leaving WordPad, like this:

1. Double-click the map object. The screen looks as shown here: ←——— Editing embedded objects

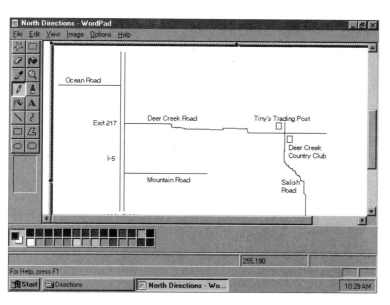

As you can see, the menu bar has changed, and the window has many of the characteristics of a Paint window, even though the title bar shows that you are still in WordPad.

2. If you know how to use the Eraser and Text tools, change Ocean Road to Ocean Avenue. (If you don't, use the Pencil tool to make a squiggle. You just need to see that when you embed an object, you can change it using the program that created it, even though the object is now stored in another document.)

3. Click outside the graphic's frame, save the document, and then close WordPad.

Embedding an object as an icon

Instead of embedding the map as a graphic object, you can embed it as an icon. Follow these steps to see the difference:

1. Open the South Directions document, press Ctrl+End to move to the end of the document, press Enter a couple of times, type *Double-click the icon below if you want to see a map:*, and press Enter twice.

2. Choose Object from the Insert menu and with Bitmap Image selected as the object type, select the Create From File option.

3. Use the Browse dialog box to find the Map graphic, double-click it to return to the Insert Object dialog box with the document's address in the File edit box, click the Display As Icon check box, and click OK. Here's the result:

What exactly are you editing?

When you make changes to an embedded object (one that is not linked to its source document), you are changing the version of the object that is stored in the open container document. Your changes do not in any way affect the original source document.

Creating new objects

When you choose Object from the Insert menu, you have the option of creating a new object of the specified type. For example, if the Map graphic did not already exist, clicking OK in the Insert Object dialog box with the Create New option and Bitmap Image selected would display a frame in the open North Directions document, and Paint's menus and tools would appear. You could then draw the map object directly in the frame. Clicking outside the frame would remove Paint's menus and tools but leave the map object in place as part of the document. You could edit the map later by simply double-clicking it to redisplay Paint's menus and tools.

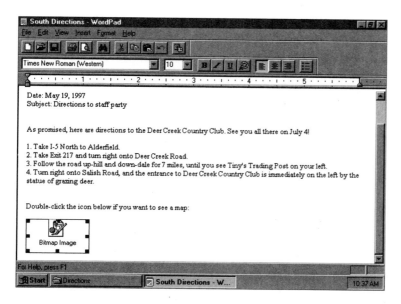

4. Save the document and then double-click the icon. A Paint window opens displaying nothing but the map. Notice that the original Map graphic was not affected by the changes you made to the map object in the North Directions document. (See the tip on page 138.)

5. Choose Exit & Return To South Directions from the File menu to return to your document.

6. Close the WordPad window.

Now let's link the map to two different documents, first as a graphic object and then as an icon:

Linking an object

1. Open the East Directions document, press Ctrl+End, press Enter a couple of times, type *Here is a map:*, and press Enter twice.

2. Choose Object from the Insert menu, and with Bitmap Image selected in the Object Type list, select the Create From File option, and click Browse. Double-click the Map graphic, and back in the Insert Object dialog box, click the Link check box, and click OK.

3. Scroll upward to see the map in place, and then save the document.

Linking an object as an icon

4. Open the West Directions document, press Ctrl+End, press Enter a couple of times, type *Double-click the icon below if you want to see a map:*, and press Enter twice.

5. Choose Object from the Insert menu and with Bitmap Image selected as the Object Type, select Create From File and click Browse. Double-click the Map graphic, and back in the Insert Object dialog box, click both the Link and Display As Icon check boxes and click OK. A shortcut icon to the Map graphic now appears at the bottom of the document.

6. Save the document and close the WordPad window.

Updating links

Now suppose that Exit 217 should be Exit 216. Because the map in the East Directions and West Directions documents is linked to the source Paint document, you can edit the Map graphic in Paint and the change will be reflected in the two linked documents. Follow these steps:

1. Double-click the Map graphic icon in the Directions folder to open the map in Paint. Use the Eraser and Text tools to make the necessary changes (or make a squiggle or two with the Pencil tool), save the map, and close Paint.

2. Open the East Directions document and scroll the window.

3. If the linked object doesn't reflect the changes you made to the Paint document, choose Links from the Edit menu to display this dialog box:

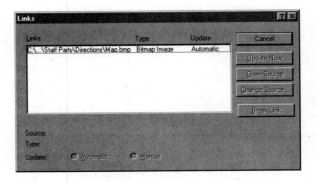

4. Select the link to the Map graphic, click Update Now, click Close, and then save the document.

5. Now open the West Directions document and double-click the Map icon. You move to a Paint window with the new version of the map displayed.

6. Tidy up the desktop by closing all open windows.

Depending on the programs you are using, you will find that OLE sometimes doesn't work quite as well as you would like. Or you will find that it works well under certain circumstances, such as when the source document is open, and not so well under others, such as when the source document is closed. However, if you need to create dynamic documents that contain objects from different programs, it is worth taking the time to experiment with OLE so that you understand how it works in the particular programs you use.

That's it for this chapter on efficiency. Hopefully, being aware of some of the possibilities will help you make your time at the computer more productive.

6

Communicating with
Windows NT Workstation 4

We cover several ways of communicating. First we show you how to use Exchange for company e-mail and Chat for on-screen conversations. Then we look at ways to communicate with the outside world, using the Internet, Phone Dialer, and HyperTerminal.

Microsoft Internet Explorer 4 makes it easy to find the information you need

Access any Web site by typing its address here

Use Outlook Express to manage both company and Internet e-mail

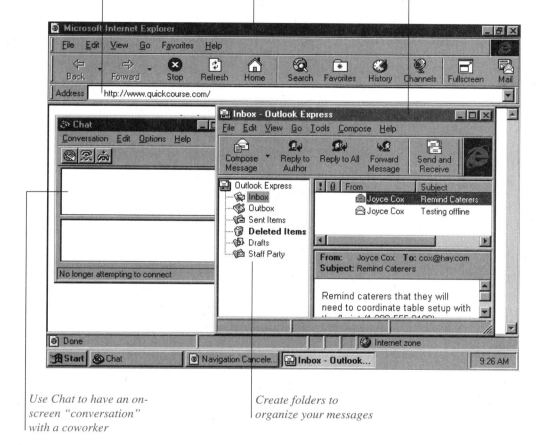

Use Chat to have an on-screen "conversation" with a coworker

Create folders to organize your messages

People don't usually work in isolation. Even if you are using Windows NT Workstation 4 on a stand-alone machine, you probably use your computer to communicate with the outside world in one way or another. In the first section of this chapter, we look at ways of using NT to communicate with coworkers within a company; our stand-alone readers can skip this section. Then we quickly explore ways of communicating with the broader community.

Communicating Within the Company

One of the great things about a network is being able to communicate electronically with your colleagues. Big deal, you might say. What's wrong with walking down the hall and using the old-fashioned method, person to person instead of computer to computer? And, of course, there's nothing wrong with it—unless the person you need to talk to is tied up in meetings all day or is otherwise unavailable for a traditional conversation.

Advantages of electronic communication

Electronic communication can lighten your load by enabling you to deal with important business right away. You don't have to scribble a note—which will probably get buried under other important notes—to remind yourself to tell a designer who is on vacation about a minor change in a product's specifications. Using Microsoft Exchange, you can dash off a quick message that will be stored in the designer's electronic mailbox and delivered when she turns on her computer. You can also use the Chat utility to make the electronic equivalent of a phone call to a colleague. In this section, we take a look at both of these communication tools.

Using Company E-Mail

Microsoft Exchange

Windows NT Workstation 4 comes with the Microsoft Exchange program, which is the backbone for a set of services called Windows Messaging. Incorporated into Exchange is Microsoft Mail, the electronic equivalent of interoffice mail. Used wisely, electronic mail (e-mail) can increase efficiency and reduce the amount of paper floating around your office, but without a little restraint, e-mail can add unnecessarily to the burden of information overload. For example, if you get in the habit of copying messages to your entire department, everyone will feel obliged to spend time reading your messages whether or not they actually need to. And if everyone prints out those messages for future reference, you'll actually increase the number of sheets of paper languishing in seldom-consulted manila file folders, rather than decreasing it. Bear in mind this potential for misuse as we see how to use e-mail.

Setting Up

In order for the people on your network to send and receive mail, the network administrator has set up a computer as the network's *post-office server*. All messages go to their recipients via the post office, and to be able to deliver messages successfully, the post office must store information about the e-mail accounts of all network users in a post-office folder. The post office is managed by a "postmaster" using a special administrator account, which can add and delete e-mail accounts and change account information (except the password).

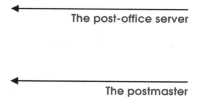

The post-office server

The postmaster

Although the postmaster usually creates an e-mail account for you on the post-office computer, the task of actually setting up e-mail on your own workstation may have been left to you. So let's start with the steps for setting up an account for Exchange. If your e-mail account is already up and running, skip to page 149. If you are using either Outlook 97 (a component of Microsoft Office 97) or Outlook Express (a component of Internet Explorer 4), see the tip below.

About Outlook

Microsoft Outlook was first introduced as part of the Microsoft Office 97 suite. It is used to manage the crucial personal and business information that you might keep in an assortment of address books, appointment books, and notebooks, as well as to handle e-mail. Outlook consists of several components that include Mail, Calendar, Contacts, Tasks, and Journal. Each component works well with other components, as well as with the application programs that comprise Office 97, which helps you streamline your daily work tasks. The Mail component of Outlook includes the Inbox, Outbox, Sent Items, and Deleted Items folders, just like Exchange (see page 155). Outlook Express is a scaled-down version of regular Outlook that includes only the Mail component. As you will learn later in the chapter, using either version of Outlook is useful because you can manage both company e-mail and Internet e-mail in one Inbox.

Assuming that your postmaster has already set up an e-mail account for you and you have access to the Windows NT Workstation 4 installation files, proceed as follows:

1. Ask your postmaster for the path of your post-office folder, the name and password for your account, and your Internet Mail account information. (You will need this information during setup.)

The Inbox icon

2. Double-click the Inbox icon on your desktop. Microsoft Exchange asks you to confirm that you want to install the Windows Messaging services.

3. Click Yes and if necessary, follow the instructions for inserting the Windows NT Workstation 4 CD-ROM and copying files to your hard drive.

The Microsoft Exchange Setup Wizard

4. When the activity on your desktop subsides and the taskbar indicates that no programs are active, double-click the Inbox icon again. This time, the Microsoft Exchange Setup Wizard starts, and you see this dialog box:

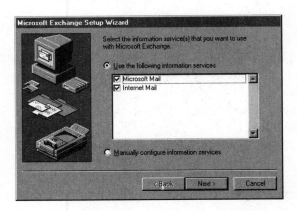

5. Click Next to set up both e-mail services.

6. In the wizard's next dialog box, enter the path of your post-office folder, which should have a name like *wgpo0000*, and click Next. You then see a dialog box like this one:

7. Select your name from the list and click Next:

8. Enter your password, click Next, and when Exchange displays a message about setting up TCP/IP for Internet e-mail, click OK. You then see this dialog box:

Changing your e-mail password

You can change your password at any time by choosing Microsoft Mail Tools and then Change Mailbox Password from the Tools menu. Enter your old password, enter the new password, confirm the new password, and click OK.

9. Select whichever connection method you will use for Internet e-mail and click Next.

10. In the next four dialog boxes, specify either the name or IP address of your Internet e-mail server; whether you will manually or automatically send and receive Internet e-mail messages (unless you are connected via a network, you will probably want to go the manual Remote Mail route); your e-mail address and your name; and your mailbox name and password.

11. When you click Next after filling in these dialog boxes, the wizard asks for the path to your Personal Address Book. If you do not already have an address book from a previous e-mail installation, click Next to accept the default path.

12. Now you need to specify the path to your Personal Folders, where your messages will be stored. Again, if you are not upgrading from an existing e-mail program, click Next to accept the default path.

13. Not far to go now. Simply tell the wizard whether you want to add Exchange to your Startup folder and click Next to display this final dialog box:

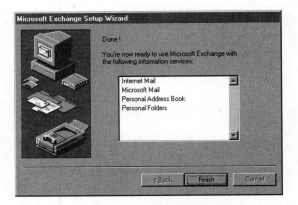

14. Click Finish. Exchange starts, and you see the window shown at the top of the facing page.

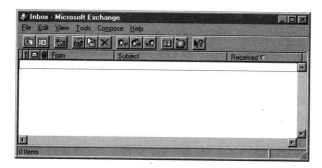

Sending and Receiving Messages

Exchange handles all e-mail messages through the window now on your screen, whether they were sent by a colleague down the hall or a client on the other side of the world. We'll look at the sending side of the equation first. For this example, imagine that you are arranging the facilities for the staff's Independence Day party and you want to remind yourself to confirm the rental of the country club first thing tomorrow morning:

1. Click the New Message button on the toolbar to open this New Message window:

The New Message button

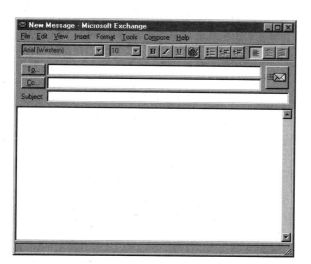

If Microsoft Word is available on your computer, Exchange loads Word's New Message window so that you can use its menus and toolbars to format your message.

E-mail etiquette

Your company may have its own *do*s and *don't*s, especially for communications with customers, but some general rules apply when sending any e-mail message. Don't compose messages in all lowercase or all uppercase letters. The former is hard to read, and the latter is considered rude. (Sending rude messages is called *flaming*.) To add flavor (tone) to your messages, you may want to use *emoticons* (sometimes called *smileys*), which are combinations of characters that look like faces when viewed sideways. But be careful: this practice can be tiresome when over used.

2. In the To edit box, type your e-mail address and press Tab. (To send a message to someone else, enter his or her address. To send the same message to more than one person, enter their addresses one after the other, separated by semicolons.)

Sending courtesy copies →

3. To send a courtesy copy of the message, you can enter the name of the recipient in the Cc edit box. For this message, press Tab to leave the Cc edit box blank.

4. In the Subject edit box, type *Confirm Rental* and press Tab.

5. Next, enter the message itself in the blank area at the bottom of the window. Type *Check on Deer Creek Country Club rental (555-0100). Be sure to tell them the caterers will be there at 4:00 PM to set up.* Your screen now looks like this:

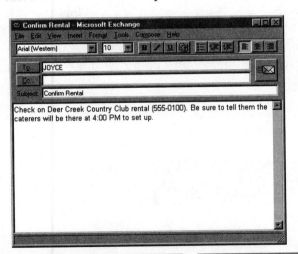

Checking addresses

Exchange underlines known addresses and changes addresses that are close to those in the Post-office Address List or your Personal Address Book. When you send a message to an unknown address, Exchange displays the Check Names dialog box so that you can create an address book entry for the name or change it. You can also display this dialog box by clicking the Check Names button on the toolbar.

Blind copies

With courtesy copies, the addresses of the original and the copy recipients are displayed. You can hide addresses by sending a *blind copy*. Choose Bcc Box from the View menu and enter the secret address(es) in the Bcc edit box. Don't abuse this feature. Although it has its uses, it is sometimes viewed as devious and can have a negative impact on your relationships with your colleagues.

Message options

The Save Sent Messages option is selected by default. You can change this setting by choosing Options from the Tools menu and making adjustments in the Options dialog box. You can also use the buttons on the New Message window's toolbar (displayed by choosing Toolbar from the View menu) to request a return receipt for the message and set the message priority to Normal, High, or Low.

6. Send the message by clicking the Send button. The New Message window closes, and the message is on its way.

The Send button

7. Minimize the Inbox window.

If you receive a message while Exchange is running, a letter icon appears in the notification area to the left of the clock on the taskbar. When you see the icon, follow these steps:

1. Double-click the letter icon to display the Inbox, which now looks like this:

The letter icon

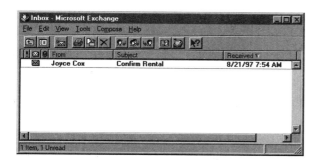

The new message is displayed in bold to indicate that you have not yet read it. The sender's name, the subject, and the date and time the message was received are all summarized, and icons tell you more about the message:

- **Urgency.** An exclamation point means a message is urgent, and a down arrow means the message is not urgent.

- **Read status.** Bold type indicates you haven't read the message, while normal type indicates that you have. The status bar at the bottom of the window tells you how many of your messages you haven't yet read.

- **Attachment.** A paper clip indicates that a file is attached to the message.

2. Double-click the summary to see the message shown on the next page.

Attaching files

To send a file with a message, you can click the Attach button in the New Message window. Locate the file you want to send in the dialog box that appears and click Attach. The attached file appears in the message as an icon. Double-click the icon to open the file in the program that created the file. (If you don't know whether the recipient has the correct program and version, save it in a generic format, such as RTF.)

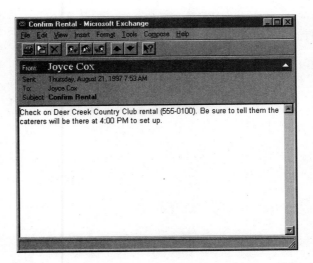

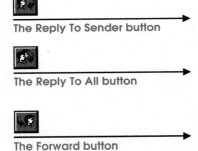

The Reply To Sender button

The Reply To All button

The Forward button

If this message was from a colleague and required a response, you could simply click the Reply To Sender button to open a RE: window with the To and Subject edit boxes already filled in. (To send the response to the sender of the message and all recipients of courtesy copies, click the Reply To All button.) Type your reply above the copy of the original message and then send the message with a click of the Send button.

To forward the message to a colleague, click the Forward button in the window containing the message. When you see the FW: window with a copy of the message already in the message area, enter the name of the person to whom you want to forward the message in the To edit box, and click Send.

3. Click the Close button to return to the Exchange window.

Shortcuts for Addressing Messages

The Postoffice Address List

If you work in a large company, you may not know everyone's exact e-mail name. To help you quickly address your messages, the post office maintains a Postoffice Address List that is accessible from the Exchange and New Message windows. Follow these steps to see how to use this list while composing a message:

1. Click the New Message button on the toolbar and click the To button to the left of the the first edit box. You see this Address Book dialog box:

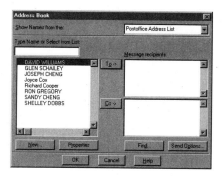

2. If the list on the left contains more names than will fit in the list box, scroll to find the name you want. Then click the name to select it. (If you know the name's first few characters, type them to scroll automatically to that general vicinity.) For this example, select your own name.

3. Now click the To button to transfer the name to the To list in the Message Recipients section, or click the Cc button to transfer it to the Cc list. You can select other names and click To or Cc to add additional recipients (the names are automatically separated by semicolons).

4. Click OK to close the dialog box and to add the selected e-mail name to the To edit box.

5. Click the Close button to close the New Message window without sending the message, and then click No to confirm that you want to discard the message.

If you send mail only to some of the people listed in the Postoffice Address List, you can create a Personal Address Book that includes only those people. Here's how:

Your Personal Address Book

1. Click the Address Book button on the toolbar to display the Address Book dialog box.

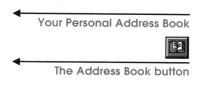

The Address Book button

2. To add a name to your Personal Address Book, select the name in the Postoffice Address List and click the Add To Personal Address Book button.

The Add To Personal Address Book button

3. To see your Personal Address Book, click the arrow to the right of the Show Names From The box and select Personal Address Book from the drop-down list. Your list replaces the post office's list.

If you often send messages to the same people, you can speed up the process by creating a Personal Distribution List:

The New Entry button

1. Click the New Entry button on the toolbar to display the dialog box shown here:

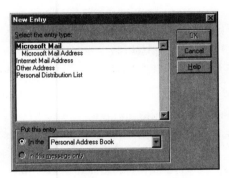

2. Check that the In The option is set to Personal Address Book, and then double-click Personal Distribution List to open a dialog box where you can define the list:

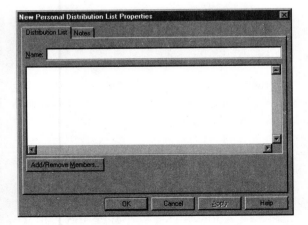

Other Address Book options

The Address Book dialog box that appears when you click the To or Cc button in the New Message dialog box includes the Properties, Find, and Send Options buttons. If you select an item in the dialog box and click Properties, Exchange displays the properties for that item. If you click Find, you can search for a specific name in the address book list. Finally, if you select a name in the To or Cc box and click Send Options, you can specify options for sending the message to the selected name.

3. Assign the list a name in the Name edit box; for this example, type *Sales*. Then click Add/Remove Members to display a dialog box similar to the one shown on page 153.

4. As a demonstration, select your own name from the Postoffice Address List and click Members to add yourself to the list. (Normally, you would add several members.) Then click OK twice to return to the Address Book dialog box.

5. If necessary, select Personal Address Book from the Show Names From The drop-down list. As you can see, the list is now accessible from the Address Book dialog box:

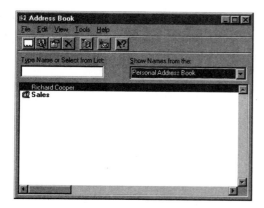

6. Select the Sales list name and click the New Message button. A New Message window opens with the selected name already in the To box. Type a subject and brief message.

7. Click the Send button and then close the Address Book dialog box. After a short while, the message sent to the Sales list shows up in your Exchange window.

Managing Your Messages

When you first start Exchange, the program creates four Personal Folders to help organize your messages: Deleted Items, Inbox, Outbox, and Sent Items. You can move messages between the folders and create new folders. Try this:

1. Click the Show/Hide Folder List button to divide the Exchange window into two panes, as shown in the graphic on the next page.

The Show/Hide Folder List button

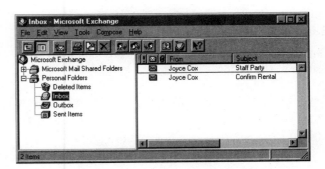

2. To see messages you have already sent, click the Sent Items folder in the left pane. The messages you have sent are summarized in the right pane.

The Delete button

3. Select the first message and click the Delete button. Then select the second message and drag it to the Deleted Items folder in the left pane. The Sent Items folder is now empty.

4. Now click the Deleted Items folder. The messages are now stored in this folder and will remain there until you quit Exchange. If you decide you want to keep one of these messages after all, you will have to drag it to another folder before you quit.

To organize your mail, you can create folders for storing related correspondence. For example, here are the steps for creating a new folder in which to store messages related to the staff party:

1. Click Personal Folders, choose New Folder from the File menu, type *Staff Party*, and click OK.

2. Click the Inbox folder, select the *Confirm Rental* message that you sent to yourself earlier, and drag its icon to the new folder.

We'll leave you to experiment with folders as you receive mail from your colleagues. Right now, we'll briefly show you how to change the look of the Exchange window to make it easier to identify and work with messages. Follow these steps:

Sending courtesy copies to yourself

Because every message you send is stored in the Sent Items folder, you might think you don't have to Cc yourself on important messages. However, when you send yourself a courtesy copy, the message has to be properly handled by the post office in order for it to show up in your Inbox. You can then be reasonably sure the message will reach the person to whom it is addressed. If it doesn't show up in your Inbox, you know something went wrong and you can resend the message or communicate in a different way.

1. Widen the Exchange window until it is almost as wide as the screen. (You can also maximize the window.)

2. Point to the dividing line between the two panes, hold down the left mouse button, and when the pointer changes to opposing arrows, drag to the left to make the right pane wider.

← Widening panes and columns

3. Adjust the widths of the From and Subject columns by dragging the dividing lines between the column headers until you can see the entire Received column in the message summary (the Size column will still be out of sight).

4. Drag any remaining messages from the Inbox folder to the Staff Party folder, and click the Staff Party folder to display its contents. Notice the down arrow in the Received column, which indicates that the messages are sorted in ascending order from bottom to top with the most recently received message at the top:

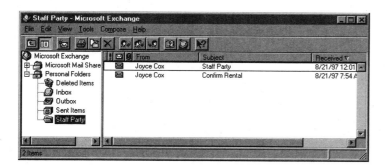

5. Click the down arrow. The messages are now sorted on the Received column in descending order, and the down arrow changes to an up arrow.

6. Click the Subject header. When the up arrow jumps to this column, clicking the arrow will sort the messages on the Subject column in ascending order. (It sorts alphabetically, but doesn't count FW: or RE: as independent words.)

Obviously, you can't see the impact of sorting with the couple of messages we have created so far. You will probably want to experiment with ascending and descending sorts on the From, Subject, and Received columns when you have received more messages.

Other ways of viewing messages

On the View menu, you can explore several other ways in which to view your messages. For example, if you choose the Group By command, you can sort your messages by up to four different fields and decide whether to sort each field in ascending or descending order. (To restore the messages to the original order, redisplay the Group By dialog box and select None from the first Group Items By edit box.) To complete a simple one field sort, choose the Sort command. To display only the messages that meet a certain criteria, choose the Filter command. In the Filter dialog box, you can enter filter criteria in the From, Sent To, Subject, or Message Body edit boxes. For example, to locate any messages sent by Joyce Cox, simply type *Joyce Cox* in the From edit box and click OK. To remove a filter and redisplay all messages, display the Filter dialog box, click Clear All and then click OK. You can add columns, such as Sensitivity or Keywords, to the message summary in the right pane by choosing Columns from the View menu, selecting a name from the Available Columns list, clicking Add, and then clicking OK. You can also use the Columns dialog box to change the order and size of the columns.

Getting On with Other Work

If you want to quit Exchange after you've sent and read your messages, you can simply close its window. However, if you are running programs that need to communicate with your colleagues or if you want to receive messages immediately after they are sent, you will want to leave Exchange running in the background while you work on other tasks. (Messages are stored by the post office if Exchange is not open or your computer is turned off.) If you are continuing directly on to the next section, complete this step:

1. Click the Minimize button to shrink Exchange to an icon.

Chatting

To round out this section on communicating within your company, we'll play with Chat. You use Chat to converse with colleagues by typing in a window. (Using Chat is like talking on the phone, whereas using Exchange is like sending a letter.) Follow these steps to chat with a coworker:

1. Choose Programs, Accessories, and Chat from the Start menu to open a window like this one:

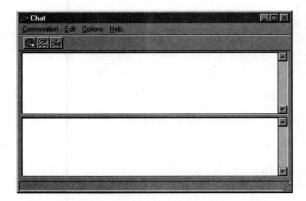

You use the top pane of the Chat window to type your half of the conversation. Your colleague's half is displayed in the bottom pane.

The Makes A Call button

2. Click the Makes A Call button on the toolbar to initiate the call. You see this dialog box:

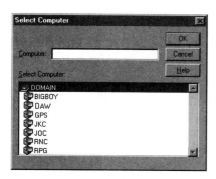

3. Double-click your colleague's computer. A message at the bottom of the Chat window indicates that Chat is dialing the computer, which has beeped to catch your colleague's attention. To make the connection, he or she must now switch to Chat, either by clicking the telephone icon displayed at the bottom of his or her screen or if the Chat window is open, by clicking the Answers An Incoming Call button on the toolbar. When the Chat window is displayed on your colleague's screen, the message *Connected to (name)* appears at the bottom of the window on both computers.

The Answers An Incoming Call button

4. In the top pane, type *Any idea when you'll be finished with your review?* or some other appropriate inquiry. The reply appears in the bottom pane.

5. To end the call, click the Hangs Up button on the toolbar.

The Hangs Up button

6. If you want to quit Chat, close its window; otherwise, click the Minimize button to run the program as an icon while you continue with your work.

Communicating with the Outside World

Company e-mail is a boon to large and small companies alike, but electronic communication is no longer confined by company boundaries. In this section, we demonstrate how the Internet and Internet e-mail can keep us in touch with vendors and suppliers on the other side of town, the continent, and the world. In addition, we cover a couple of handy communications utilities that come with Windows NT Workstation 4.

Using the Internet

Once people get used to communicating with coworkers via e-mail, traditional methods of communication start to feel cumbersome. How come you can dash off a quick electronic note to Dianne way over in Building 22 but you have to word process, print, and mail a letter to Ms. Dalton at Northwest Printing, which is virtually next door? Fortunately, many of us now have access to the Internet, which brings the ease of company e-mail to communications outside the company. But that's not the only benefit of Internet access. We can now efficiently disseminate and obtain information outside the company via the Internet component known as the World Wide Web, and we can disseminate and obtain information inside the company by setting up a Web look-alike called an *intranet* (see the tip below).

What You Need

To take advantage of the Internet services available with Windows NT Workstation 4, you need the following:

- **TCP/IP.** A protocol for transferring information over the Internet, must be installed on your computer.

- **A Web browser.** Microsoft Internet Explorer (which comes with NT) or another browser must be installed on your computer.

- **A modem.** Or you must be able to access a network modem. (You install a modem on your own computer by using the Modem icon in Control Panel.)

- **Internet access.** You or your company must have an account with an Internet service provider (ISP), or your company must provide Internet access.

- **Dial-Up Networking.** If your Internet access is via an ISP and through a modem connected to your own computer, you must have Dial-Up Networking installed, and you must set up a Dial-Up Networking connection so that your computer can talk to the ISP's computer over phone lines.

- **Internet proxy server.** If your Internet access is via your network, you need to give NT information about the proxy server (available from your network administrator).

Intranets

Using Internet technology, many companies are setting up Internet servers and creating intranets that are accessible only from the company's computers (no matter where they are physically located). The intranet enables people to easily and cheaply access company information, exchange ideas, and collaborate on projects. A system of security "firewalls" ensures that the intranet information is available only to the people in the company who are authorized to access it, not to general Internet users.

The technical details of installing the necessary tools is beyond the scope of this book, and you should enlist the help of your network administrator or your ISP in getting everything set up just right. Once you have a working Internet connection established, you can join us for the next section, where we use Internet Explorer to take a quick look at the Web.

Using Internet Explorer

To surf the Internet or a company intranet, you can use Microsoft's Web browser program, Internet Explorer, which comes with Windows NT Workstation 4. We can't do more than briefly introduce you to Internet Explorer here, but what we do cover should give you enough information for you to be able to explore further on your own. Let's fire up Internet Explorer and check it out:

1. If necessary, connect to your Internet service provider.

2. Double-click the Internet Explorer icon on your desktop to start the browser (or just click if you have updated your desktop; see page 163). After some initial activity, Internet Explorer displays its starting page, which is the home page of Microsoft's Web site:

The Internet Explorer icons

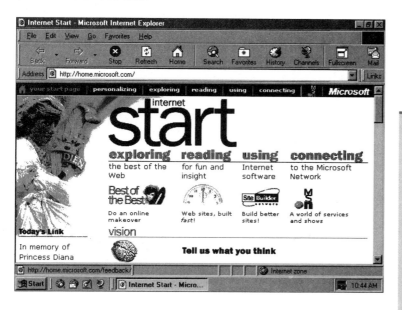

Service Pack 3

To run Internet Explorer 4, you must have Service Pack 3 installed on your computer. Microsoft releases service packs from time-to-time to update the operating system (fix bugs and patch security holes) and improve performance. You can download Service Pack 3 from Microsoft's Web site (*www.microsoft.com*) or you can order it on CD-ROM by calling (800) 426-9400.

Your program window will look different from ours if you are running a version of Internet Explorer other than version 4. The viewing area will also look different because Microsoft changes this Web site frequently.

Checking the URL

3. The first thing to do is to check that we are all looking at the same Web site. Check that the entry in the Address box matches ours. (This entry is called a *universal resource locator*, or *URL*; see below for more information.) If your entry is different, click the current entry to select it, type *http://home.microsoft.com/*, and press Enter.

Checking the version

4. Next, check which version of Internet Explorer is installed on your computer. If you didn't notice the version when Internet Explorer started, choose About Internet Explorer from the Help menu, make a note of the version, and then click the Close button.

The Internet Explorer Updates button

If you are not running Internet Explorer 4 (or later), you can download the latest version of the browser from Microsoft's Web site. If you are running version 2, clicking the Internet Explorer Updates button takes you to an area of the site where you can accomplish this task. If you are using version 3, look for a Products link or a linked headline that extols the virtues of the latest (and of course greatest) release. Then find a link that will allow you to obtain the latest version, click it, and follow the instructions. Rejoin us when your upgrade is complete.

Confused by all the terms we've used so far? We assume you know what the Internet and the World Wide Web are, but here's a quick run down of four other terms:

- **Web site.** An informational resource published by a government agency, company, organization, or individual on the World Wide Web. Sites can consist of text, graphics, and multimedia components such as audio and video files, all coded in such a way that they can be viewed by Web browsers.

- **URL.** The address of a Web site. To better understand URLs, we can break down an address, such as *http://www.quickcourse.com*, into its component parts. The *http* component of a URL address stands for *HyperText Transfer Protocol*, which is the name for the set of rules used on the Web. Next, comes the *domain name*, which is the name of the computer (or *server*) on which the Web resource is stored. Domain names of servers in the US usually end in *com* for a company, *edu* for an educational institution, *gov* for a government agency, *mil* for a military agency, *net* for network administration support, and *org* for another type of organization.

- **Home page.** The starting point of a Web site. (For ease of viewing, the information stored at a Web site is divided into chunks called *pages*.)

- **Links.** You can move from one page to another within a Web site—and even from site to site—by clicking *hyperlinks*, which are coded addresses of related information attached to text or other elements on a page.

Now let's see these elements in action. Web sites can change dramatically over time, and frequently sites that are here today are gone tomorrow. For purposes of demonstration, we'll take you to the Quick Course Web site and show you around. Follow these steps:

1. Click the URL in the Address box to select it.

Moving to another Web site

2. Now type *www*, then a period, then *quickcourse.com*. Check that the entire entry now reads *www.quickcourse.com* and press Enter. Because the URL begins with *www*, Internet Explorer adds *http://* in front of it. (You have to type *http://*

Active Desktop

When you install Internet Explorer 4, you are given the option of updating your desktop so that it works like a Web page. Desktop icons then resemble hyperlinks, requiring only a single click to take you where you want to go. You can move back and forth the way you do between Web pages. To turn on Active Desktop, right-click your desktop and choose Active Desktop and then View As Web Page from the object menu. (If this command is not available, you need to install Windows Desktop Update. Activate your Internet connection and then open Control Panel. Double-click Add/Remove Programs, click Microsoft Internet Explorer 4.0, click Add/Remove, and then click Add Windows Desktop Update From Web Site. You can then turn on Active Desktop.

for URLs that don't begin with *www*.) After a flurry of activity, Internet Explorer displays this Quick Course home page:

As you'll see, reading the information at a Web site is not like reading a book. Follow the steps on the next page to get a feel for how Web information is organized and how to move around.

Moving within a Web site

1. Move the pointer over the row of graphics below the title, noticing that the pointer changes to a hand to indicate that the graphics are hyperlinks (don't click anything yet).

2. Scroll through the home page using the scroll bar and move the pointer over the underlined words, noticing how the pointer changes to a hand over these text hyperlinks.

3. Scroll to the top of the home page, point to the *Catalog* graphic hyperlink, and with the pointer shaped like a hand, click the left mouse button. Your screen now looks like this:

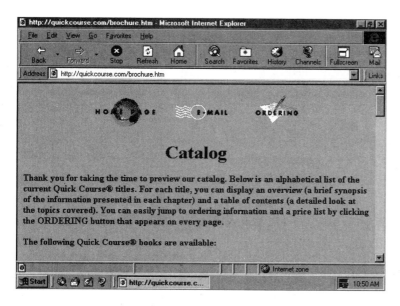

4. Scroll the title list until you see *Quick Course in Office 97*, and click the *Overview* text hyperlink to jump to a new page.

   Suppose we want to go back to the title list to check out a different book. Internet Explorer provides two buttons on its toolbar that we can use to move backward and forward through the pages we have already displayed, no matter which Web site those pages belong to. Try this:

1. Click the Back button on the toolbar to redisplay the catalog page, then click Back again to redisplay the home page.

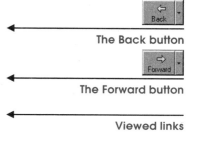

The Back button

The Forward button

Viewed links

2. Click the Forward button to redisplay the catalog page, and notice that the *Overview* hyperlink for the *Quick Course in Office 97* title has changed color to remind you that you have already viewed the information on that page.

3. Scroll to *Quick Course in Microsoft Internet Explorer 4*, and click its *Overview* hyperlink. (If you are interested in learning about the browser in more detail than we present here, you might want to check out this book.)

   Some Web pages provide hyperlinks we can use to move directly from one part of the site to another. Turn the page to check this out.

Jumping to the home page

1. Scroll to the bottom of the Internet Explorer Overview page and click the Home Page graphic to move directly back to the Quick Course home page, the first page of this Web site. (Most well-designed sites include a hyperlink back to the home page from all the other pages in the site.)

2. Scroll the home page, click the *frequently asked questions* hyperlink, and then click the first question, *What is a Quick Course® book?* This is what you see:

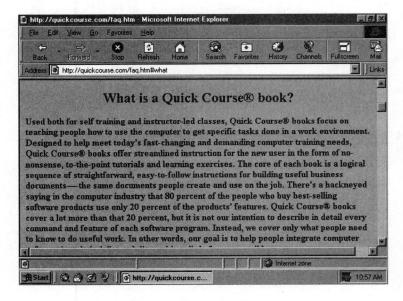

3. Click the Back button and then scroll the page. Notice that the page contains the list of questions at the top, followed by the answers. The hyperlinks we used previously all jumped to a linked file (a different page) that is stored at the same Web site, whereas each question hyperlink jumps to a linked place within the same file (the same page).

Frequently asked questions (FAQs)

So many Web sites include a frequently asked questions page that these pages have become known as *FAQs*. Clicking a hyperlink labeled *FAQ* usually takes you to a list of common questions and answers, so this is a good place to start when you are looking for information.

4. Continue testing the hyperlinks at the Quick Course Web site until you can move around with ease, and then click the Home button on the toolbar to display Internet Explorer's starting page, shown earlier on page 161.

5. If you have been collecting the addresses of Web sites you want to check out, enter one of them in the Address box and explore another Web site now. (Remember, if you get lost, click the Home button to come back to familiar territory.)

The Internet Start page provides ways of finding information on the Web, as well as information about Microsoft products, and you will want to explore its many features on your own. Here, we want to show you another way of tracking down the information you need. To do research on the Web, we can search a Web database—a collection of information about Web sites and their content. Several databases are available, but we'll take a look at only Yahoo here. Because the techniques for searching are pretty similar for all the databases, you'll be able to check out the others on your own later. For now, follow these steps:

Web database

1. Type *www.yahoo.com* in the Address box and press Enter to jump to Yahoo's home page, which is shown here:

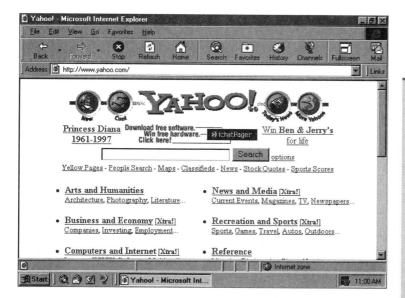

How are Web databases built?

Web databases are built using a variety of methods. Some rely totally on a program called a Web crawler that electronically crawls through the Web gathering information about the sites it finds; others use a Web crawler but also encourage Web-site owners to submit information about their sites for inclusion in the database. (You might hear people talk about worms, spiders, or robots, which are types of crawlers.) Some are comprehensive and include everything; others focus on specific types of information. Some do little more than organize the information into categories; others add site reviews and ratings. Because of these construction differences, one database doesn't necessarily contain the same information as another.

2. Ignore the Search box at the top of the page and scroll through the available categories, noting their subcategories for future searches.

3. Under *Regional*, click *U.S. States*. Then scroll the page and click your state.

4. On the state page, click *Cities*. Then click your city (or the closest one). Yahoo displays information about the area in which you live.

Using the Back list

5. Click the arrow to the right of the Back button and select *Yahoo!* from the drop-down list.

6. Scroll to the bottom of the Yahoo home page, click *Weather Forecasts*, click *United States*, click your state, and click your city to see the weather for your area.

7. Again, click the arrow to the right of the Back button and select *Yahoo!* from the drop-down list to return to the Yahoo home page.

Suppose you want to search for information about digital cameras and you haven't a clue which category to look in. You can use a keyword search instead of a category search to track down the information. Try this:

Constructing keyword searches

To get meaningful results from a Web search, you have to construct your search criteria very carefully to narrow down the results as much as possible. For example, if you want to locate information on climbing gyms in Boise, you might try typing *Boise climbing gyms* as your search criteria. However, the results of the search would give you Web sites containing the words *Boise* or *climbing* or *gyms*—possibly more than 50,000 sites! To search on the exact string of the words *Boise climbing gyms*, enclose the text in double quotation marks (" "). If you want to find sites that contain both the phrase *climbing gyms* and the word *Boise*, but not necessarily together, you can type *+Boise+"climbing gyms"*. The plus sign tells the search engine that the results must contain the following word(s). To exclude a word, type a minus sign.

1. At the top of the Yahoo home page, click an insertion point in the Search edit box, type *digital+cameras*, and click the Search button. Then click Yes when Internet Explorer displays a Security Alert dialog box. Yahoo searches through its database for the keywords you entered and displays the results.

2. Scroll through Yahoo's findings (called *hits*), clicking the hyperlinks of any that look promising.

When it's time to end an Internet session, the procedure we use will depend on our Internet service provider. In our case, quitting Internet Explorer leaves us still connected to our provider, so quitting the program and logging off our account are two separate procedures. In the steps on the next page, substitute whatever procedure is appropriate for your setup.

1. Click the Close button at the right end of the Internet Explorer title bar to quit the program.

2. Right-click the modem icon at the right end of the taskbar, choose Hang Up and then your ISP from the object menu, and click Yes to sign out of your Internet account.

Using Internet E-Mail

In this section, we discuss using e-mail for direct, two-way communication with other Internet users. In our examples, we use Outlook Express, the mail program that comes with Internet Explorer 4, but you will easily be able to apply our instructions to any other mail program you might want to use. The advantage of using Outlook Express is that once it is set up, you can send and receive both Internet and company e-mail from the same inbox, instead of having to use different programs for the different types of e-mail.

Outlook Express

If you are associated with a large organization, Internet e-mail has probably already been set up on your computer. If it hasn't, you may need to tell your mail program where you want it to store your mail, your name, your user name, the domain names of the servers that will handle your outgoing and incoming messages, and how you access the Internet before you can send or receive e-mail. (See the tip on the next page for hints about setting up Outlook Express.)

Once everything is set up correctly, sending, receiving, and managing Internet e-mail is not much different from dealing with company e-mail. To see what's involved, let's quickly compose and send a message using Outlook Express. For this example, suppose we want to remind ourselves to check with the company that is catering the Independence Day staff party first thing tomorrow morning. Follow these steps:

1. Connect to your ISP and start Outlook Express by clicking its icon. You see this window:

The Outlook Express icon

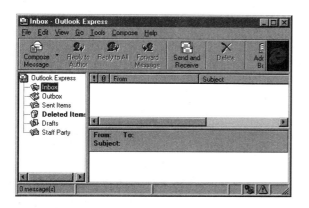

As you can see, the left pane of the window lists your folders, the top right pane will hold your message summaries, and the bottom right pane is where you'll read your messages.

The Compose Message button

2. Click the Compose Message button on the Outlook Express toolbar to display this New Message window:

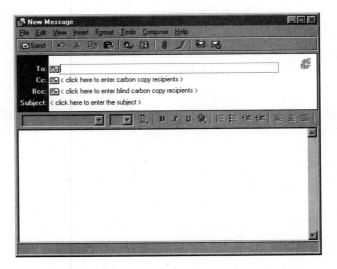

Setting up Outlook Express

To set-up Outlook Express, double-click the Mail-Windows Messaging icon on the desktop. With the Start Outlook Express And Make It Your Default Mail Client option selected, click OK. When you see the Browse For Folder dialog box, click OK to accept the default (notice that this folder is part of your user profile; see page 133). You then see the first Internet Connection Wizard dialog box. Follow the wizard's instructions and then click Finish. Next follow the Outlook Express Import wizard's instructions. The first time you use Outlook Express, you'll be asked to specify how you want to connect to the Internet; otherwise, you're done!

3. In the To box, type your own Internet e-mail address and press Tab three times. (To send a message to someone else, you type his or her address. To send the same message to more than one person, you type their addresses one after the other, separated by a comma and a space.)

4. In the Subject box, enter *Remind Caterers* and press Tab.

5. Type the following message in the message area:

Remind caterers that they will need to coordinate table setup with the florist (1-800-555-0100).

Your screen now looks like this one:

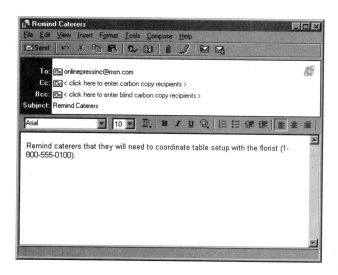

6. Send the message by clicking the Send button on the toolbar. ←

The Send button

Usually, we will want to keep Outlook Express open while we work on the Internet so that we can receive any new messages. Here's how to manually retrieve the message we just sent to ourselves:

1. Click the Send And Receive button on the toolbar. ←

The Send And Receive button

2. Outlook Express retrieves your message, and the window now looks like this:

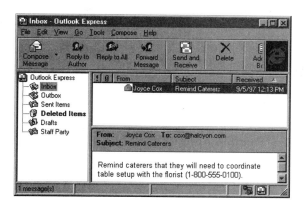

You might also see messages from the Microsoft Outlook Express Team welcoming you to Outlook Express or alerting you to other issues. (We've adjusted the width of the left pane and the columns in the top right pane.)

Working offline

You can work offline by starting Outlook Express without connecting to the Internet. In the Outlook Express window, choose Work Offline from the File menu. Then write your message, clicking the Send button as usual. If Outlook Express tells you that your message will be stored in the Outbox, click OK. When you have finished all your correspondence, choose Work Offline from the File menu again, and then click the Send and Receive button. If you are connected to the Internet via an ISP, Outlook Express prompts you to establish the connection. It then sends your messages on their way.

The Reply To Author button

Here's how to read and reply to a message:

1. With the Remind Caterers message displayed in the message area, Click the Reply To Author button on the toolbar to open a Reply window where the To and Subject boxes are already filled in. (You can also click Reply To All.)

2. Select and delete the original message and type *Thanks for the reminder!*

3. Click the Send button to send the reply on its way.

We'll leave you to explore Outlook Express further. In particular, you might want to test your knowledge of shortcut ways of addressing messages and organizing your messages in folders. As you'll see, having one universal inbox where you can handle all your e-mail is a great convenience, and it's worth spending some time getting to know the lay of the land.

Dialing Phone Numbers

At the low-tech end of modem communications is Phone Dialer. This program, which comes with NT, dials any of eight stored numbers in response to a button click. It can also be used to manually dial any number. To use Phone Dialer, you need a modem connected to your computer and a telephone connected to your modem. Then follow these steps:

1. Click the Start button, point to Programs, point to Accessories, and click Phone Dialer to display this window:

Using your computer as a fax machine

As of this writing, no fax program is included with Windows NT Workstation 4. However, a beta of a simple fax product for NT is available for downloading from Microsoft's Web site. Go to *www.microsoft.com/ntworkstation/fax.htm and register.* You need Service Pack 2 or later to use it. As with all beta products, be prepared for bugs, integration problems, and not-yet-working features.

2. Click the 1 button in the Speed Dial section to display this dialog box:

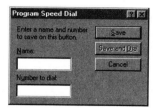

3. Type *800 Numbers* in the Name edit box, type *1 (800) 555-1212* (with spaces before the open parenthesis and after the close parenthesis) in the Number To Dial edit box, and click Save.

To dial the number, all you have to do is click the 800 Numbers button. You can then pick up the phone receiver, click the Talk button, and continue the phone call as usual. (This is a useful number to know, but don't actually place the call unless you genuinely need a specific 800 number. We don't want to frivolously increase the workload of some poor 800 Directory Inquiries operator.)

Dialing with speed buttons

Now follow these steps to manually dial a number:

1. In the Phone Dialer window, click the buttons corresponding to the phone number or extension of a colleague, exactly as you would push the buttons on a touchtone phone.

Dialing manually

2. Click Dial, pick up the phone receiver, click the Talk button, proceed with the call as usual, and then hang up.

3. Close the Phone Dialer window.

Using HyperTerminal

Windows NT Workstation 4 comes with the HyperTerminal program, which enables you to connect your computer, via modems and phone lines, to other computers. The principal use for HyperTerminal is for private computer-to-computer file transfers and for connecting to local computer bulletin board systems (BBS's). Bulletin boards exist in most communities, large and small, and usually focus on specific interests. Users can post notes, exchange information, carry on

Bulletin boards

computer "conversations," and so on, often for modest membership fees. (Some government agencies and corporations use free bulletin boards to provide information about their services and products, but these have largely been superceded by Web sites.)

Here's how to connect to another computer or a BBS:

Connecting to another
computer or bulletin board

1. Click the Start button, point to Programs, point to Accessories, point to Hyperterminal, and click HyperTerminal to display this dialog box:

2. Type a name for the computer or BBS you are connecting to in the Name edit box, scroll the Icon bar and select an appropriate icon, and click OK to display the dialog box shown on the top of the next page.

3. Change the area code if necessary, type the phone number, and click OK to display this dialog box:

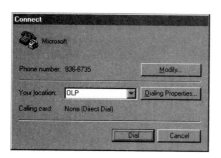

4. Click Dial to tell your modem to connect to the computer at the specified number.

5. When you want to disconnect, click the Disconnect button on the toolbar and then click the Close button. HyperTerminal asks whether you want to save this session.

The Disconnect button

6. Click Yes if you want to be able to connect to this computer or BBS again without having to reenter all the connection information, or click No to discard the information.

If you save the session, a shortcut for the computer or BBS is added to the HyperTerminal submenu. You can then simply choose this entry to open the connection and click Dial.

7

Changing Your Computer's Setup

NT has a set of useful tools you can use to tailor your computer to your own way of working. We first cover taskbar customization, and then we show you how to make common adjustments and briefly discuss less common ones.

*Customize the taskbar
in a variety of ways*

*Use Control Panel icons
to tailor your computer
setup to the way you work*

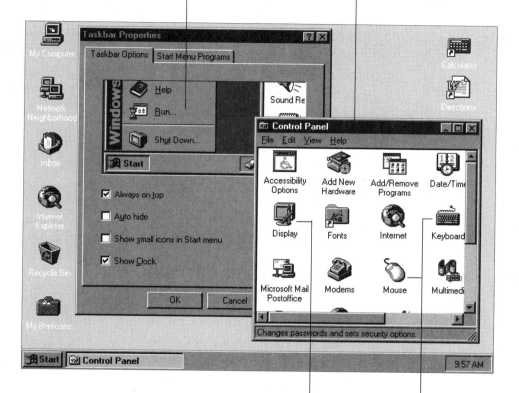

*Change screen colors,
run a screen saver,
and make other display
adjustments*

*Change the mouse
and keyboard
response rates*

In this chapter, we give you a brief overview of the Windows NT Workstation 4 tools you can use to customize the look of your display, change your computer's setup, and add new programs. We've left this discussion until Chapter 7 because we feel you are unlikely to need these tools when you first start using NT. Moreover, if you are working on a network, your network administrator may not allow you to make some changes. No matter what your particular situation, you can glance through this chapter to learn about the available options. Then if you're allowed to experiment, you'll know where to start.

Most of the tools we cover in this chapter are grouped in the system folder called Control Panel. As you know, this folder is accessible via My Computer and Windows NT Explorer, but the easiest way to open it is as follows:

1. Click the Start button, choose Settings from the Start menu, and click Control Panel to display the window shown way back in Chapter 1 on page 20.

2. Minimize the Control Panel window.

Before we explore Control Panel's tools, we'll take this opportunity to show you how to change the way the taskbar appears on your screen.

Customizing the Taskbar Display

As you have seen while working through the examples in this book, the Start menu and the taskbar are important elements of the NT interface. Because you use them so frequently, you can customize them for maximum convenience. You learned how to add and remove Start menu items in Chapter 5 (see page 120). Here, we'll look at ways to manipulate the entire taskbar.

Although the taskbar is located at the bottom of your screen by default, it doesn't have to stay there. Try this:

Relocating the taskbar

1. Point to the taskbar, hold down the left mouse button, and drag to the top of the screen. When you release the mouse button, the taskbar jumps into place, as shown here:

2. Now drag the taskbar to the right side of the screen. NT adjusts the width of the bar so that you can see the entire Start button.

3. Drag the taskbar back to the bottom of the screen. When you release the mouse button, the taskbar returns to its original size.

   As well as moving the taskbar around, you can use the Taskbar Properties dialog box to change its look. Follow these steps:

1. Right-click the taskbar and choose Properties from the object menu to display this dialog box:

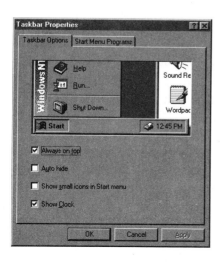

Changing taskbar properties

Changing the height of the taskbar

If you open many programs and their buttons become so crowded on the taskbar that you can't easily distinguish them, point to the taskbar's top border (assuming it is in its default location) and when the pointer changes to a two-headed arrow, drag upward to double the taskbar's height. The buttons then spread themselves out, stacking themselves in two rows.

2. On the Taskbar Options tab, click the Always On Top option to deselect it, and notice that the window on the right in the illustration above is now over the taskbar.

3. Click the option again to turn it back on, and notice that the taskbar is now over the window. (You will probably want to leave this option selected so that the taskbar is always at hand.)

Hiding the taskbar → 4. Click the Auto Hide option and notice that the taskbar has disappeared from the illustration. This option is useful when you want to display as much of your document as possible on the screen.

5. Click OK to close the dialog box.

6. Point to the bottom edge of the screen, and the taskbar pops up. Move the pointer elsewhere, and the taskbar hides itself.

7. Display the taskbar, click the Start button, and choose Settings and then Taskbar from the Start menu to redisplay the Taskbar Properties dialog box.

8. Click the Auto Hide option to turn it off.

The Taskbar Options tab provides a couple of other ways of tailoring the taskbar. Try this:

Changing the Start menu's icons → 1. Click the Show Small Icons In Start Menu option, noticing the effect in the illustration above. Then click it again. As you can see, small icons take up less room and large icons are easier to identify. Finish with whichever setting you prefer.

Turning off the clock → 2. Toggle the Show Clock option on and off, noticing the effect in the illustration. (You might want to turn off the clock if you have many windows open and you want to make room for their buttons on the taskbar.)

3. Check that all the taskbar customization options are as you want them and click OK to close the dialog box.

4. Back at the NT desktop, click the Control Panel button on the taskbar to display its window.

You can now double-click any icon in the window to access the tools for changing other aspects of your computer's setup. In the following sections, we don't deal with the tools in the order in which they appear, and we don't deal with some of the more techie ones at all. But by the end of the chapter, you'll have a good idea of what's available to you.

Adding or Removing Programs

Setting up a program to be used under NT is not simply a matter of copying the program to your hard drive. Usually the program comes with a setup program that makes sure all the necessary pieces are copied to the correct locations and alerts NT to its existence. If you later remove the program, not only must the program's files be deleted from your hard drive, but ideally NT should remove all references to the program from its system files. Similarly, if you add or remove any of the programs that come with Windows NT Workstation 4, NT needs to be involved so that it can take care of the necessary housekeeping.

Adding or Removing Application Programs

To install a new application program from a floppy disk or CD-ROM, double-click the Add/Remove Programs icon in the Control Panel window to display this dialog box:

The Add/Remove Programs icon

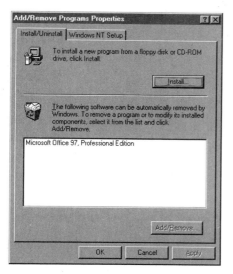

The Install Wizard

Insert the first installation disk or the CD-ROM and click the Install button to start the Install Wizard. The wizard searches your floppy drive and CD-ROM drive for an installation program and then prompts you to confirm that it should run the program. When you click Finish, the installation program takes over from the Install Wizard, prompting you for any information it needs.

If the application program comes with an uninstall utility, the Install Wizard adds the program to a list of uninstallable programs. If you want to remove the program, you can select it from the list box at the bottom of the Install/Uninstall tab of the Add/Remove Programs Properties dialog box, and then click the Add/Remove button. If the program you want to remove is not listed, look for an uninstall application in the folder where the program is stored. (It will most likely be labeled *Remove* or *Uninstall*.) If you don't find anything there, check the program's documentation or call tech support for that particular program.

Adding or Removing NT Components

When Windows NT Workstation 4 was installed on your computer, the person responsible for the installation could pick and choose among various NT components. As a result, it is unlikely that you have all the programs that come with NT on your computer. As you work with NT, you may find you need a program that was not initially installed, or you may find you never use a program that was installed. With NT, you can add or remove certain components at any time, provided you have permission to change your computer's setup in this way.

To add or remove NT components, first double-click the Add/Remove Programs icon in the Control Panel window and then click the Windows NT Setup tab of the Add/Remove Programs Properties dialog box to display the options shown at the top of the facing page.

AutoPlay

If you have a CD-ROM drive and use reference materials provided on CD-ROM, you'll probably be interested in the AutoPlay feature. *AutoPlay* simply means that when you insert a CD-ROM in your CD-ROM drive, NT assumes you want to use that CD-ROM immediately without you having to do anything. (Only CD-ROMs that have been produced since the release of Windows 95 in August 1995 can take advantage of this feature.)

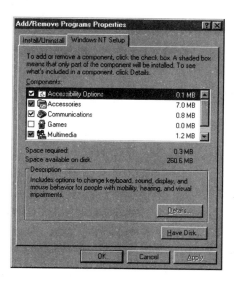

In the Components list box, NT displays the optional components by category. Categories with all components installed display a ✔ in a white check box, while categories with only some components installed display a ✔ in a gray check box. If a category has more than one component, NT tells you how many components in the selected category are currently installed and how many are available. On the right side of the Components list, NT displays how much hard disk space the installed components for each category use.

To add or remove an entire category, click the check box to the left of the category's name. (Clicking an empty check box puts a ✔ in the box and adds the category; clicking a check box with a ✔ removes the ✔ and removes the category.) Turn the page to see how to add or remove a component.

Adding/removing categories

Adding or removing hardware

If you are allowed to add new hardware to your computer, such as a sound card or modem, you will need to tell NT about any new devices. Similarly, if you remove a device from your computer, you'll want to tell NT that the device is no longer available. Look for options in the corresponding Control Panel tools to add or remove hardware or to change the configuration of your existing hardware. Any new device must be listed in NT's Hardware Compatibility List, or if it was developed after the release of Windows NT Workstation 4, you must have a driver specifically designed for NT. This driver is a control program that enables NT to work with the device. If necessary, contact the device's manufacturer and ask for a Windows NT 4 driver and instructions for installing it. A word of warning: don't play around where NT and devices are concerned. Unless you know what you're doing, leave any changes to the experts.

1. Click the Accessories category name and then click the Details button to display this dialog box:

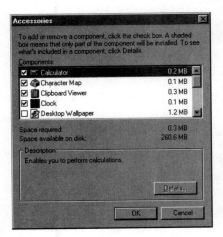

Desktop wallpaper

2. If there is no ✔ in the Desktop Wallpaper check box, click the check box to add that component.

3. Click OK to close the Accessories dialog box, and then click OK again to close the Add/Remove Programs Properties dialog box. If you aren't allowed to add NT components, you see this message box:

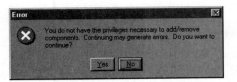

4. Click No, deselect Desktop Wallpaper in the Accessories category, and click OK twice.

Customizing the Way You Work

With Windows NT Workstation 4, you rarely need to live with a setting that annoys you or interferes with your work. Does the color of your screen bother you? Do you want to switch the left and right mouse buttons or change the keyboard repeat rate? Then this section is for you. We'll explore two categories of customization: first, the options you are most likely to want to change and are most likely to be able to experiment with; and second, the options that you are unlikely to want to change and that only experienced users should mess with (provided, of course, that they have the proper permissions).

Common Adjustments

The options covered in this section are fairly easy to change, and experimenting with them can't harm your system. As you follow the instructions in our examples, bear in mind that you can actually implement a change by clicking OK in a dialog box, or you can leave the current setting as it is by clicking Cancel. If we give instructions for something you can't do, simply skip that section.

Changing the Date or Time

As you have seen, the time is displayed at the right end of the taskbar, and the date is displayed in a pop-up box when you point to the time with the mouse. If you have permission, you can use the Date/Time icon in the Control Panel window to set your computer's date and time. Or you can right-click the clock at the right end of the taskbar and choose the Adjust Date/Time command from the object menu. Let's try the second method:

The Date/Time icon

1. Move the pointer to the clock at the right end of the taskbar and right-click it.

2. Choose Adjust Date/Time from the object menu. Windows displays this dialog box:

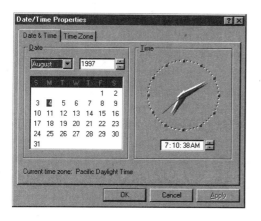

Bold object-menu commands

When you right-click an object on the NT desktop, you'll often notice that one command on the object menu appears in bold. If you simply double-click the object, the bold command is carried out automatically. For example, when you right-click the clock, the Adjust Date/Time command, which opens the Date/Time Properties dialog box, appears in bold on the object menu. If you double-click the clock instead, the Date/Time Properties dialog box appears automatically.

3. In the Date/Time Properties dialog box, click the arrow at the right end of the Month box and select January from the drop-down list.

4. In the Year edit box, click the spinner's up arrow until the year changes to 1998.

5. On the calendar, click Thursday, the 1st.

6. If the time needs adjustment, select the hour, minutes, seconds or AM/PM in the Time edit box and type a new entry. (You can also select each component of the time and use the spinner arrows to change it.)

Changing the time zone

7. If you want to change the time zone, click the Time Zone tab to display this map:

8. Select the zone you want from the drop-down list.

9. Assuming you don't really want to change the date, time, and time zone, click Cancel to close the Date/Time Properties dialog box without making any changes.

Tailoring the Display

The Display icon

You can adjust the look of your screen by changing its color scheme, resolution, screen saver, and other visual settings. You can access these settings by double-clicking the Display icon in the Control Panel window, but the fastest way to make adjustments to your display is to do the following:

1. Point to a blank area of the desktop and click the right mouse button.

2. Choose Properties from the object menu to open this Display Properties dialog box:

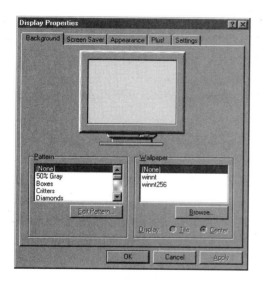

On the Background tab of the dialog box, you can easily change the pattern of your desktop. If you want something fancier, NT comes with several bitmap graphics files that you can use to *wallpaper* the desktop. (Large and colorful wall-paper files can really eat up memory, so if you're low on memory, you might want to skip the wallpaper.) Let's change the pattern of the desktop and then wallpaper it:

1. In the Pattern section, click the various pattern names in the list and notice their effect on the sample screen shown above the list. When you have finished exploring, select Thatches and click OK.

Changing the background

2. Right-click an empty section of the desktop again and then choose Properties from the object menu to redisplay the Display Properties dialog box.

3. In the Wallpaper section of the Background tab, click all the available wallpaper names and notice their effect on the sample screen. (If the Desktop Wallpaper component of the NT

Accessories category isn't installed, Winnt and Winnt256 are the only choices.) When you're ready, select Winnt256.

4. At the bottom of the Wallpaper section, select the Tile option to fill the entire desktop with tiled copies of the wallpaper graphic, and then click OK. Notice that the wallpaper completely obscures the Thatches pattern you selected earlier.

5. Assuming that you don't like your screen's new look, redisplay the Display Properties dialog box and try a different background, or return both the Pattern and Wallpaper settings to (None).

In the Display Properties dialog box, you can also specify whether NT should display a moving picture or pattern during periods of screen inactivity. A moving display helps prevent static screen objects, such as window title bars and menu bars, from "burning into" the monitor, and also hides your work-in-progress from passersby if you take a break. Here's how to activate a screen saver:

Displaying a screen saver →

1. Open the Display Properties dialog box and click the Screen Saver tab to display these options:

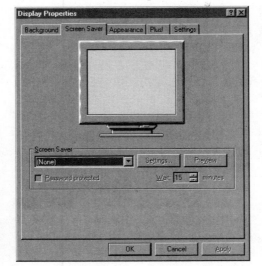

Using other screen savers

You can display a screen saver program that you've purchased or downloaded, by using the Add/Remove Programs icon (see page 181) in the usual way. Then you activate the screen saver by double-clicking the Display icon in Control Panel and selecting it from the drop-down list on the Screen Saver tab.

2. Click the arrow at the right end of the Screen Saver box and select 3D FlowerBox from the list of options. The sample

screen shows what the screen saver looks like, but you can also click the Preview button to see its effect full-screen. (After you click the Preview button, moving the mouse returns you to the Display Properties dialog box.)

3. Watching the flying objects might give you motion sickness, so click the Settings button to display this dialog box:

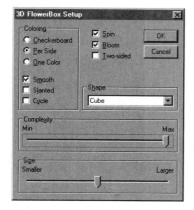

4. Experiment with the options in this dialog box, clicking OK to view their effects in the Display Properties sample screen. Click OK a final time when the screen saver looks the way you want it.

5. In the Wait edit box, use the spinner to specify 5 minutes as the period of inactivity after which NT should turn on the screen saver. Then click OK to apply your changes and close the dialog box.

To make the screen as easy as possible on your eyes, you can change the colors of standard NT elements, such as the scroll bars, the active title bar, and the desktop. Change the color scheme now by following these steps:

1. Open the Display Properties dialog box and click the Appearance tab to display the options shown on the next page.

Scrolling marquees

NT provides a screen saver called Marquee Display that shows text on your screen when the screen saver is activated. You can use this feature to remind yourself of an important event or a task that needs to be completed during the day. (Obviously, the computer must be turned on and idle for the screen saver to be activated.) To create a marquee screen saver, double-click the Display icon in Control Panel and then click the Screen Saver tab. Select Marquee Display from the Screen Saver drop-down list and click the Settings button to display the settings options. Here, you can type your text in the Text edit box (for example, Don't forget Joyce's *birthday!*) and then adjust the position and speed of the marquee and the background color of the screen. You can click the Format Text button to change the font, size, or color of your marquee text.

2. Click the arrow to the right of the Scheme box and select Desert from the list of preset color schemes. In the window above the list, NT displays a sample of what the color scheme will look like.

3. To change the color of the active title bar, click the arrow to the right of the Item box, scroll the list, and select Active Title Bar. Then click the arrow to the right of the Color box and select navy blue (the second option in the fourth row of the color palette).

4. While you're at it, try changing the font of the active title bar by selecting Times New Roman from the Font drop-down list. (You can also change the size, color, and other attributes of the font.)

5. Click OK to implement your changes or click Cancel to ignore them and leave the current settings in place.

Playing with colors can be fun, and we encourage you to experiment with this feature to learn more about it. We also recommend that you choose colors that are easy on the eyes, especially if you use NT a lot. After experimenting, you can always return to the default color scheme by selecting Windows Standard from the Scheme drop-down list.

Adjusting the Mouse

You can change how fast you have to double-click the mouse button or make other adjustments to the mouse by using the Mouse icon in the Control Panel window. Here's how:

The Mouse icon

1. In the Control Panel window, double-click the Mouse icon to display this dialog box:

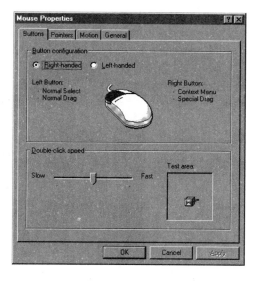

2. On the Double-Click Speed slider on the Buttons tab, drag the indicator to the left to slow down double-clicking (in other words, to allow you to take more time between clicks and still have NT recognize the action as a double-click).

Changing the double-click speed

3. Test your adjustment by double-clicking the Test Area jack-in-the-box. Jack jumps up when you double-click the box at the correct speed. (Double-click again to tuck Jack back in the box.)

4. Make any necessary adjustments to the speed, and when you're ready, click OK to close the dialog box.

You can also change the button configuration on the Buttons tab. If you are a southpaw and find it easier to click and

Switching the buttons

highlight text with the right mouse button instead of the left, select the Left-Handed option in the Button Configuration section. The switch takes place as soon as you click OK. Obviously, you would then "right-click" with the left mouse button to display an object menu.

Changing the pointer scheme

If NT's Mouse Pointers component is installed on your computer, you can click the Pointers tab of the Mouse Properties dialog box and select a different set, or scheme, of pointers. Some of the schemes are simply more attractive than the standard set, some are entertaining, and some are downright cutesy. You can design your own scheme by selecting an event in the list box, clicking the Browse button, selecting a pointer to represent the event, and clicking open. When you have specified pointers for all the events in the list box, you can save the scheme by clicking the Save As button and naming the set.

Changing the pointer speed

On the Motion tab of the Mouse Properties dialog box, you can change the pointer speed and have the mouse pointer automatically move to the default button in dialog boxes.

Installing a new pointing device

If you change the type of pointing device attached to your computer, you can tell NT about it on the General tab. If you are working on a network and don't have permission to add and remove hardware, the Change button on this tab is not available.

Adjusting the Keyboard

If your keyboard repeats characters faster than you would like it to or if the insertion point blinks too fast or too slow, you can make adjustments in the Keyboard Properties dialog box. Let's experiment:

The Keyboard icon

1. With the Control Panel window displayed on your screen, double-click the Keyboard icon to display this dialog box:

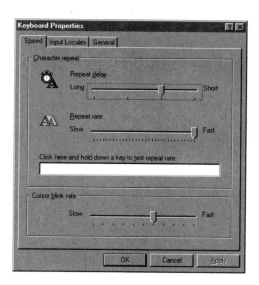

2. The Repeat Delay slider determines how long NT waits before starting to repeat a key you are holding down. Drag the indicator all the way to the left to make the repeat delay as long as possible.

3. The Repeat Rate slider determines how rapidly NT repeats the key after the initial delay. Drag the indicator all the way to the left to make the repeat rate as slow as possible.

4. Test your changes by clicking an insertion point in the Click Here edit box below the Repeat Rate slider and holding down any character key. As you'll see, NT now responds very slowly to this keyboard action.

5. Adjust the Repeat Delay and Repeat Rate sliders until you find a speed to suit your typing style.

6. If you want, change the cursor blink rate by adjusting the slider at the bottom of the dialog box.

7. Click OK to close the dialog box.

Adding or removing fonts

You can use the Fonts folder in Control Panel to add fonts for use with NT programs such as Word-Pad and Paint. Choose Install New Font from the File menu, select the drive and location of the font, and click Install. To see a sample of a font, double-click the font's icon in the Fonts folder window. To print the sample, click the Print button and click OK in the Print dialog box. Each font uses a small amount of memory and disk space. If you think you won't use a particular font, you can use the Fonts folder to remove it. Right-click it in the Fonts dialog box and choose Delete from the object menu. Be careful not to delete a font that came with NT, because if NT uses that font in a menu or a dialog box, the text will disappear.

The Accessibility Options icon

Changing the Accessibility Options

If you have a physical condition that makes using the computer difficult, you might want to check out the Accessibility Options icon in the Control Panel window. Double-clicking this icon displays the dialog box shown here:

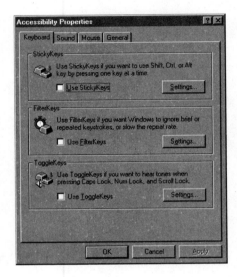

Among other options, this multi-tabbed dialog box allows you to specify the following:

Keyboard options

- **StickyKeys.** You can press the Ctrl, Alt, or Shift keys and have them remain active until you press a key other than Ctrl, Alt, or Shift. This feature is designed for people who have difficulty pressing more than one key at a time.

- **FilterKeys.** You can instruct the computer to ignore accidental or repeated keystrokes. (You can also adjust the keyboard repeat rate to avoid this problem, as we just did.)

- **ToggleKeys.** The computer will emit one tone when you turn on the Caps Lock, Scroll Lock, or Num Lock key and another tone when you turn any of these keys off.

Sound options

- **SoundSentry.** You can specify that visual warnings be displayed whenever your computer makes a sound.

- **ShowSounds.** You can tell the programs you use to display captions for any speech or sounds they make.

- **MouseKeys.** You can commandeer the numeric keypad to control your mouse pointer.

  Mouse options

- **SerialKeys.** You can attach alternative devices to the computer's serial port if you cannot use a standard keyboard or mouse.

  Other input devices

You might want to explore the various sections of this dialog box to get a feel for the many accessibility options that are available.

Uncommon Adjustments

In the previous section, we discussed adjustments you might make to the NT environment so that your work on the computer is easier and more pleasant. In this section, we'll cover adjustments you will rarely or perhaps never make. You may want to just skim through this section, coming back to specific parts if you need to later. A word of warning: even if you can, don't tamper with the features covered in this section unless you are confident that you know what you're doing. If you have any doubts, consult someone with more computer experience before making a change.

Setting Mail Options

By double-clicking the Mail And Fax icon in the Control Panel window, you can change settings for Microsoft Exchange, which handles e-mail (see page 144 for more information). Unless you are familiar with Microsoft Exchange, we suggest leaving all of the default options in place.

The Mail And Fax icon

Setting the Internet Proxy Server

Double-clicking the Internet icon displays a dialog box in which you can specify a proxy server for internet access. (You can get the necessary information from your network administrator.)

The Internet icon

Fine-Tuning Your Modem Configuration

You can adjust the setup of your modem by double-clicking the Modems icon in the Control Panel window. In the Modems Properties dialog box, you can add or remove a modem,

The Modems icon

change properties such as the port or the volume of the speaker, and change dialing properties. As with the e-mail configurations, we recommend leaving the modem configuration as it is, unless you are familiar with your modem and how it operates.

Setting Multimedia Options

The Multimedia icon

If you have multimedia accessories on your computer, such as a sound card and speakers, you can make adjustments to the setup by double-clicking the Multimedia icon in the Control Panel window. In the multi-tabbed Multimedia Properties dialog box, you can alter the audio, video, MIDI (for *Musical Instrument Digital Interface*), and CD Music properties, depending on which accessories are installed on your computer. If you have permission, you can also add new multimedia accessories by using options on the Devices tab. Most likely, you won't need to make any adjustments in this dialog box. However, if you have a multimedia computer, you might want to take a look at the available options.

Configuring a Network

The Network icon

Unless you have general experience with computers and specific experience with your network, another icon to avoid in the Control Panel window is the Network icon. In the Network dialog box, you can change your computer name and domain or workgroup affiliation, and change the way your computer accesses the network. You can also add or remove a network adapter and change its setup. On a client-server network, most likely you will be allowed to view the current configuration but not change it.

Changing Regional Settings

The Regional Settings icon

When you double-click the Regional Settings icon in Control Panel, NT displays the Regional Settings Properties dialog box. Selecting a region from a drop-down list on the Regional Settings tab changes the way programs display and sort numbers, currency, times, and dates. (Changing the region doesn't affect the language used in menus and dialog boxes.) You can also customize the display of these elements on the corresponding tabs of the dialog box. For example, if you prefer to display the day before the month in dates, you can click the Date tab. Then click the arrow to the right for the Long Date Style box, select *dddd, dd MMMM, yyyy* from the drop-down list, and click OK.

Playing Sounds

The Sounds icon

If you have a sound card, you can use the Sounds icon in the Control Panel window to assign sounds to system and application events. In the Name drop-down list in the Sounds Properties dialog box, you can select a sound that came with NT (or one you have installed or created) and then link it to a specific event, such as when you exit NT or empty the Recycle Bin. You can "preview" a sound in the Preview section of the dialog box before you assign it.

That concludes our quick tour of NT customization options. As we said, you will probably want to experiment with the options you are allowed to change to discover the setup that best suits the way you work.

Index

Quick Course®
books—first-class training at
economy prices!

"...perfect to help groups of new users become productive quickly."
—PC Magazine

Perfect for educators and trainers, Quick Course® books offer streamlined instruction for the new user in the form of no-nonsense, to-the-point tutorials and learning exercises. The core of each book is a logical sequence of straightforward, easy-to-follow instructions for building useful business documents—the same documents people create and use on the job.

Microsoft Office 97
U.S.A.	**$24.99**
U.K.	£22.99
Canada	$34.99
ISBN 1-57231-726-4	

Microsoft Windows 95
U.S.A.	**$14.99**
U.K.	£13.99
Canada	$20.99
ISBN 1-57231-727-2	

Microsoft Word 97
U.S.A.	**$14.99**
U.K.	£13.99
Canada	$20.99
ISBN 1-57231-725-6	

Microsoft Excel 97
U.S.A.	**$14.99**
U.K.	£13.99
Canada	$20.99
ISBN 1-57231-723-X	

Microsoft Access 97
U.S.A.	**$14.99**
U.K.	£13.99
Canada	$20.99
ISBN 1-57231-722-1	

Microsoft PowerPoint 97
U.S.A.	**$14.99**
U.K.	£13.99
Canada	$20.99
ISBN 1-57231-724-8	

Microsoft Press

Take
productivity
in stride.

Things are looking up!

Here's the remarkable, *visual* way to quickly find answers about Microsoft applications and operating systems. Microsoft Press® *At a Glance* books let you focus on particular tasks and show you with clear, numbered steps the easiest way to get them done right now.

Microsoft® Excel 97 At a Glance
Perspection, Inc.
U.S.A. $16.95 ($22.95 Canada)
ISBN 1-57231-367-6

Microsoft® Word 97 At a Glance
Jerry Joyce and Marianne Moon
U.S.A. $16.95 ($22.95 Canada)
ISBN 1-57231-366-8

Microsoft® PowerPoint® 97 At a Glance
Perspection, Inc.
U.S.A. $16.95 ($22.95 Canada)
ISBN 1-57231-368-4

Microsoft® Access 97 At a Glance
Perspection, Inc.
U.S.A. $16.95 ($22.95 Canada)
ISBN 1-57231-369-2

Microsoft® Office 97 At a Glance
Perspection, Inc.
U.S.A. $16.95 ($22.95 Canada)
ISBN 1-57231-365-X

Microsoft® Windows® 95 At a Glance
Jerry Joyce and Marianne Moon
U.S.A. $16.95 ($22.95 Canada)
ISBN 1-57231-370-6

Microsoft Press

Get quick, easy answers— anywhere!

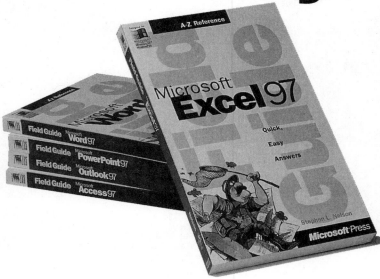

Microsoft® Excel 97 Field Guide
Stephen L. Nelson
U.S.A. $9.95 ($12.95 Canada)
ISBN 1-57231-326-9

Microsoft® Word 97 Field Guide
Stephen L. Nelson
U.S.A. $9.95 ($12.95 Canada)
ISBN 1-57231-325-0

Microsoft® PowerPoint® 97 Field Guide
Stephen L. Nelson
U.S.A. $9.95 ($12.95 Canada)
ISBN 1-57231-327-7

Microsoft® Outlook™ 97 Field Guide
Stephen L. Nelson
U.S.A. $9.99 ($12.99 Canada)
ISBN 1-57231-383-8

Microsoft® Access 97 Field Guide
Stephen L. Nelson
U.S.A. $9.95 ($12.95 Canada)
ISBN 1-57231-328-5

Microsoft Press® Field Guides are a quick, accurate source of information about Microsoft Office 97 applications. In no time, you'll have the lay of the land, identify toolbar buttons and commands, stay safely out of danger, and have all the tools you need for survival!

Microsoft Press